Robert B. Reich

Aftershock

Robert B. Reich is Chancellor's Professor of Public
Policy at the Richard and Rhoda Goldman School of
Public Policy at the University of California, Berkeley. He has served in three national administrations,
most recently as secretary of labor under President
Bill Clinton. He has written twelve books, including
The Work of Nations, which has been translated
into twenty-two languages, and the bestseller *Supercapitalism.* His articles have appeared in *The New
Yorker, The Atlantic, The New York Times, The Washington Post,* and *The Wall Street Journal.* He is also
cofounding editor of *The American Prospect* magazine. His film, *Inequality for All,* directed by Jake
Kornbluth, was released in September 2013. He lives
in Berkeley and blogs at www.robertreich.org.

ALSO BY ROBERT B. REICH

Beyond Outrage

Supercapitalism

Reason

I'll Be Short

The Future of Success

Locked in the Cabinet

The Work of Nations

The Resurgent Liberal

Tales of a New America

The Next American Frontier

AS EDITOR
The Power of Public Ideas

AS COAUTHOR, WITH JOHN D. DONAHUE
New Deals: The Chrysler Revival and the American System

Aftershock

Aftershock

THE NEXT ECONOMY AND AMERICA'S FUTURE

Robert B. Reich

Vintage Books
A Division of Random House LLC
New York

The Library of Congress has cataloged the Knopf edition as follows:
Reich, Robert B.
Aftershock : the next economy and America's future / Robert B. Reich.
Includes bibliographical references and index.
1. United States—Economic conditions—2009–.
2. United States—Economic conditions—2001–2009.
3. United States—Social conditions—21st century—Forecasting.   I. Title.
HC106.84.R45 2010
330.973—dc22
2010004134

Vintage ISBN: 978-0-307-47633-3

Author photograph © Perian Flaherty
Book design by Robert C. Olsson

www.vintagebooks.com

Printed in the United States of America
10 9 8 7 6 5 4 3

To Ella Reich-Sharpe, and her generation

Epochs of private interest breed contradictions . . .
characterized by undercurrents of dissatisfaction,
criticism, ferment, protest. Segments of the population fall behind in the acquisitive race. . . . Problems neglected become acute, threaten to become
unmanageable and demand remedy. . . . A detonat-
ing issue—some problem growing in magnitude
and menace and beyond the market's invisible hand
to solve—at last leads to a breakthrough into a new
political epoch.

—Arthur M. Schlesinger, Jr.,
The Cycles of American History

CONTENTS

PART II

Backlash

PART III

The Bargain Restored

Aftershock

INTRODUCTION

I

I've always been short for my age, which I suppose is why I was bullied as a kid more than most. Early on though, I came up with a way to ward off the bullies. I made friends with boys who were bigger and older than I was—and bigger and older than the bullies. My new friends protected me. It was my original protection racket.

Not until many years later did I make a connection between what happened to me as a child and my concerns as an adult for those who have felt helpless in an economy that too often bullies vulnerable people. Economic bullying takes many forms but almost always preys on individuals and families that have little or no power and are at the mercy of those who do.

As inequality has widened in America and in many other places around the world—with a relatively small number of people getting an increasing share of income and total wealth—many who are left behind feel vulnerable and helpless. They lose their job or their wages drop, and they can't pay their bills. Some end up losing their cars or even their homes. Many discover they can't afford to send their children to college, and don't have enough money to retire. They don't dare get sick.

Unlike me when I was bullied, these people don't have anyone to protect them. They can't count on their employer because companies are under intensifying pressure to maximize profits and share prices, and one way they do this is by cutting payrolls—laying off even more workers, reducing pay and benefits, outsourcing and subcontracting.

Most can't count on a union to bargain on their behalf because

1

union membership has declined precipitously; today, fewer than 7 percent of American workers in the private sector belong to a union.

They feel they can't depend on government because political power has shifted to the top along with the money. Money has translated into large campaign donations to politicians who do the bidding of their wealthy patrons—reducing their tax rates, widening tax loopholes, gaining government subsidies and bailouts for their businesses, and slashing regulations that impinge on them but would otherwise protect the public. That power shift has also meant less public funding for services that average families need— good schools and public transportation, adequate healthcare and affordable universities, and safety nets to catch them if they slip any further.

Let me be clear. Some inequality is inevitable; we are not born with equal talents and inherited abilities. Some inequality is also necessary if people are to have adequate incentive to work hard, invent, and innovate to the benefit of everyone.

But at some point inequality becomes so wide it undermines democracy. It also hobbles an economy by reducing overall demand. The vast middle class no longer has the purchasing power to keep the economy going, while the small group at the top that's raking in the money spends only a fraction of it, speculates with much of it, and parks the rest around the world wherever it collects the highest return at the lowest tax.

At some point inequality also makes mockery of the ideal of equal opportunity. Upward mobility in America has slowed considerably over the past few decades. It's far more likely now that a child born into a poor family will be poor as an adult and a child born into wealth will be a wealthy adult. The odds of a poor child getting ahead are lower in the United States than in the United Kingdom, despite its history of inherited aristocracy.

And at some point inequality becomes so wide it causes a society to fracture. Average people become so frustrated and fearful they become easy prey for demagogues hurling blame at anyone or any group that's a convenient scapegoat. Politics disintegrates into name-calling. History is rife with examples.

We would be wise not to wait until we reach these tipping points.

2

I wrote the first edition of this book in 2010, not long after the near-meltdown of Wall Street and ensuing Great Recession. It seemed to me that although the excesses of the Street were the proximate cause of the downturn, a deeper explanation was found in the changing structure of the economy.

For three decades before the crash, American workers had become steadily more productive—following the same upward trajectory they'd been on for the first three decades after World War II. Yet in sharp contrast to that earlier period, when the median wage rose in tandem with productivity gains, real wages had barely risen since the late 1970s. Almost all the economic gains had gone to the top.

I saw the beginning of this in the late 1970s when I was ran the policy planning staff of the Federal Trade Commission. Wage gains were slowing even as productivity continued to rise. Was it a statistical fluke or the start of a trend?

By the mid-1980s the trend was unmistakable, but its cause was unclear. In *The Work of Nations*, published in 1991, I argued that the double whammy of global competition and computer technologies had split the workforce into three groups: a small, well-educated elite whose analytic and innovative skills were in ever greater demand; a shrinking number of routine workers whose good-paying (and often unionized) jobs were going abroad or being replaced by automated machinery and computer software;

and a large and growing class of personal-service workers burdened by low pay, few benefits, and little security.

I didn't think the trend was inevitable. But reversing it required an economic strategy quite different from the one then in vogue, reflecting the prevailing faith in an omnipotent and all-knowing free market. Ronald Reagan and the first George Bush deregulated and privatized, fought labor unions, cut taxes on the wealthy, slowed investments in education and infrastructure, and shredded social safety nets. The manifest result was stagnating wages for most Americans, increasing job insecurity, and steadily widening inequality. Yet those who were doing well and who possessed the political power to reverse the troubling trend were largely indifferent to it. Socially and geographically, they were separating from the rest of the country. The "secession of the successful," I argued, was fully underway.

The vast American middle class maintained its living standards (and was able to continue to buy most of the goods and services it produced) only by sending wives and mothers into paid work and by working longer hours. The shift of women into paid jobs was one of the largest social transformations of postwar era—and it also served to mask the widening inequality. In the late 1970s, the richest 1 percent of the country took in less than 8 percent of the nation's total income. By the time Bill Clinton was elected president in 1992, the richest 1 percent was getting over 13 percent.

After his election, Bill Clinton—whom I had known since our days as graduate students at Oxford University—invited me to Washington to run his economic transition team, and then to join his cabinet as Secretary of Labor. He had read *The Work of Nations* and wanted to reverse the trend by increasing public investment in education and job training (the title of his campaign platform was "Putting People First,") and helping Americans get better jobs at higher wages.

I was elated—until I discovered that almost no one in official

Washington outside the Clinton White House shared that goal. Even the new president began losing sight of it as the ensuing economic boom further obscured the underlying trend. As a result, we didn't do enough to reverse it. The economy also turned out to be more fragile than anyone assumed. The 1990s boom ended when families could not work any more hours and when the "dot-com" bubble burst.

After the Clinton years, the middle class turned to another mechanism to maintain its living standards in the face of near-stagnant real wages. Families went into debt, using the rising values of their homes as collateral and refinancing their mortgages. But this couldn't last. When the debt bubble burst in 2008 the game was up. Most Americans finally had to confront the reality of flat or declining incomes. They had no choice but to curtail spending—fueling a vicious cycle. Without enough buyers, companies shed workers. The Great Recession began.

It is no mere coincidence that the two years in the last hundred that marked the apogees of inequality—when the richest 1 percent received a record 23.5 percent of total income—were 1928 and 2007. I don't mean to suggest that such astonishing consolidations at the top directly caused the sharp economic declines of the following years. The connection was, and is, more subtle. Without enough purchasing power, most Americans cannot keep the economy going. Borrowing has its limits and debt bubbles eventually burst. Yet the rich don't spend as much of their earnings as the rest of us. As I noted, they speculate with them and invest their savings around the world. At some point—1929 and 2008 offer ready examples—the economy becomes so top-heavy that it tips over.

In November 2008, President-elect Obama asked me to join his economic advisory board. By then the U.S. economy appeared to be in free fall. What policies should the new president pursue? Several of us suggested a large stimulus but I feared that wouldn't be enough. The economy would never fully bounce back until the trend toward widening inequality was reversed. The middle class had exhausted all the mechanisms for maintaining its spending and keeping the economy going: It couldn't send more wives and mothers into paid work; it couldn't work longer hours; it could no longer go on a borrowing binge.

I offered several ideas for how to revive middle-class wages and return to broad-based prosperity. But once again, political will was lacking. It is far easier for politicians to interpret downturns as temporary crises and administer short-term remedies than to recognize and fix more fundamental problems.

Only by dint of extraordinary effort—the Federal Reserve lowering interest rates to near zero, and Congress and the White House bailing out Wall Street and spending hundreds of billions of dollars—was the economy kept from going over the brink as it had done almost eighty years before in the Great Depression. Yet these efforts were also enough to remove pressure for fundamental reform. Apart from legislation to expand the nation's system for delivering health care to the uninsured, and subsequent legislation to raise the top income tax rate from 35 to 29.6 percent, little else was done to overcome the widening inequality and accompanying insecurity that lay at the Great Recession's core, relative to what had been done in the Great Depression. Inequality continued to widen.

As soon as it was possible, moneyed interests declared the recession over, and then lobbied intensively for cuts in the federal budget—leaving the underlying trend unaddressed. These cuts jeopardized the health and well-being of lower-income families and children, reduced investments in education and infrastructure, and slashed safety nets. If a Keynesian stimulus offered only temporary relief, austerity economics offered only temporary misery. Neither responded to the basic problem.

Countries with less inequality than in the United States also got hammered by the financial crisis of 2008. This was mainly because America's bad debt had been parceled out around the world and also because many of these countries depended on exports to America, which dropped precipitously. Notably, other rich nations with high levels of inequality, such as Great Britain, were hit especially hard. To their detriment, they embraced austerity even more thoroughly.

3

As I write this in 2013 the American economy is picking up somewhat and unemployment is down from the terrifying heights it reached during the Great Recession. But America continues to be hobbled by one of the weakest recoveries on record, and wages continue to drop, when adjusted for inflation. Real annual median household income sunk from $51,144 in 2010 to $45,018 in 2012. All the gains from the recovery continue to go to the top. Much of Europe, meanwhile, is contracting. The Japanese economy continues to languish. China's economy is slowing, as are the economies of many developing nations that are dependent on exports to China, Europe, and the United States.

Economies always rebound from declines, even from the depths of the darkest downturns. To this extent, the business cycle is comfortably predictable. Businesses must eventually reorder when inventories grow too depleted, families have to replace cars and appliances that are beyond repair, and a growing population needs houses and apartments to live in. Governments spending can fill the shortfall in private-sector spending, at least for a time. And even if governments eventually cut spending in response to yawning budget deficits, central banks supply the steroid of easy money and low interest rates.

But none of these will generate lasting prosperity and enduring growth if the fundamentals are out of whack—if most consumers aren't capable of consuming and saving, if businesses therefore have few incentives to expand and hire, if public investments are inadequate, and if income and wealth are disproportionately flowing to a smaller and smaller share of the population.

I will argue here that these fundamentals remain profoundly skewed, that the Great Recession was but the latest and largest symptom of the growing distortion, and that we—both in the United States and elsewhere—will have to choose, inevitably, between deepening discontent (and its ever nastier politics) and fundamental social and economic reform. I believe that we must—and eventually will—choose the latter.

Some say that Americans have for too long lived beyond their means and must now endure the painful adjustment of living within them—including cuts in public budgets. This view is profoundly wrong. The problem is, rather, that the means of most Americans have not kept up with what a growing economy can— and should have been able to—provide them.

This is the crux of our economic predicament. It is also our social and political predicament. We will continue to experience ugly divisiveness until we solve it. The answer is not for most Americans to lower their standard of living. It is to reorganize the American economy so that its benefits are more widely shared, as they were decades ago. Even those at the top would do better with a smaller share of a rapidly growing economy than with a large share of an anemic one and with a society less prone to divisiveness and demagoguery. Until this transformation is made our economy will continue to languish and our politics become ever more embittered.

Robert B. Reich
June 2013

PART I

The Broken Bargain

1

Eccles's Insight

The Federal Reserve Board, arguably the most powerful group of economic decision-makers in the world, is housed in the Eccles Building on Constitution Avenue in Washington, D.C. A long, white, mausoleum-like structure, the building is named after Marriner Eccles, who chaired the Board from November 1934 until April 1948. These were crucial years in the history of the American economy, and the world's.

While Eccles is largely forgotten today, he offered critical insight into the great pendulum of American capitalism. His analysis of the underlying economic stresses of the Great Depression is extraordinarily, even eerily, relevant to the Crash of 2008. It also offers, if not a blueprint for the future, at least a suggestion of what to expect in the coming years.

A small, slender man with dark eyes and a pale, sharp face, Eccles was born in Logan, Utah, in 1890. His father, David Eccles, a poor Mormon immigrant from Glasgow, Scotland, had come to Utah, married two women, became a businessman, and made a fortune. Young Marriner, one of David's twenty-one children, trudged off to Scotland at the start of 1910 as a Mormon missionary but returned home two years later to become a bank president. By age twenty-four he was a millionaire; by forty he was a tycoon—director of railroad, hotel, and insurance companies; head of a bank holding company controlling twenty-six banks; and president of lumber, milk, sugar, and construction companies spanning the Rockies to the Sierra Nevadas.

In the Crash of 1929, his businesses were sufficiently diverse and his banks adequately capitalized that he stayed afloat financially. But he was deeply shaken when his assumption that the economy would quickly return to normal was, as we know, proved incorrect. "Men I respected assured me that the economic crisis was only temporary," he wrote, "and that soon all the things that had pulled the country out of previous depressions would operate to that same end once again. But weeks turned to months. The months turned to a year or more. Instead of easing, the economic crisis worsened." He himself had come to realize by late 1930 that something was profoundly wrong, not just with the economy but with his own understanding of it. "I awoke to find myself at the bottom of a pit without any known means of scaling its sheer sides. . . . I saw for the first time that though I'd been active in the world of finance and production for seventeen years and knew its techniques, I knew less than nothing about its economic and social effects." Everyone who relied on him—family, friends, business associates, the communities that depended on the businesses he ran—expected him to find a way out of the pit. "Yet all I could find within myself was despair."

When Eccles's anxious bank depositors began demanding their money, he called in loans and reduced credit in order to shore up the banks' reserves. But the reduced lending caused further economic harm. Small businesses couldn't get the loans they needed to stay alive. In spite of his actions, Eccles had nagging concerns that by tightening credit instead of easing it, he and other bankers were saving their banks at the expense of community—in "seeking individual salvation, we were contributing to collective ruin."

Economists and the leaders of business and Wall Street—including financier Bernard Baruch; W. W. Atterbury, president of the Pennsylvania Railroad; and Myron Taylor, chairman of the United States Steel Corporation—sought to reassure the country that the market would correct itself automatically, and that the government's only responsibility was to balance the federal budget. Lower prices and interest rates, they said, would inevitably "lure 'natural new investments' by men who still had money and credit and whose revived activity would produce an upswing in the economy." Entrepreneurs would put their money into new technologies that would lead the way to prosperity. But Eccles wondered why anyone would invest when the economy was so severely disabled. Such investments, he reasoned, "take place in a climate of high prosperity, when the purchasing power of the masses increases their demands for a higher standard of living and enables them to purchase more than their bare wants. In the America of the thirties what hope was there for developments on the technological frontier when millions of our people hadn't enough purchasing power for even their barest needs?"

There was a more elaborate and purportedly "ethical" argument offered by those who said nothing could be done. Many of those business leaders and economists of the day believed "a depression was the scientific operation of economic laws that were God-given and not man-made. They could not be interfered with." They said depressions were phenomena like the one described in the biblical story of Joseph and the seven kine, in which Pharaoh dreamed of seven bountiful years followed by seven years of famine, and that America was now experiencing the lean years that inevitably followed the full ones. Eccles wrote, "They further explained that we were in the lean years because we had been spendthrifts and wastrels in the roaring twenties. We had wasted what we earned instead of saving it. We had enormously inflated values. But in time we would sober up and the economy would right itself through the action of men who had been prudent and thrifty all along, who had saved their money and at the right time would reinvest it in new production. Then the famine would end."

Eccles thought this was nonsense. A devout Mormon, he saw

that what passed for the God-given operation of economics "was nothing more than a determination of this or that interest, specially favored by the status quo, to resist any new rules that might be to their disadvantage." He wrote, "It became apparent to me, as a capitalist, that if I lent myself to this sort of action and resisted any change designed to benefit all the people, I could be consumed by the poisons of social lag I had helped create." Eccles also saw that "men with great economic power had an undue influence in making the rules of the economic game, in shaping the actions of government that enforced those rules, and in conditioning the attitude taken by people as a whole toward those rules. After I had lost faith in my business heroes, I concluded that I and everyone else had an equal right to share in the process by which economic rules are made and changed." One of the country's most powerful economic leaders concluded that the economic game was not being played on a level field. It was tilted in favor of those with the most wealth and power.

Eccles made his national public debut before the Senate Finance Committee in February 1933, just weeks before Franklin D. Roosevelt was sworn in as president. The committee was holding hearings on what, if anything, should be done to deal with the ongoing economic crisis. Others had advised reducing the national debt and balancing the federal budget, but Eccles had different advice. Anticipating what British economist John Maynard Keynes would counsel three years later in his famous *General Theory of Employment, Interest and Money,* Eccles told the senators that the government had to go deeper into debt in order to offset the lack of spending by consumers and businesses. Eccles went further. He advised the senators on ways to get more money into the hands of the beleaguered middle class. He offered a precise program designed "to bring about, by Government action, an increase of purchasing power on the part of all the people."

Eccles arrived at these ideas not by any temperamental or cultural affinity—he was, after all, a banker and of Scottish descent—but by logic and experience. He understood the economy from the ground up. He saw how average people responded to economic downturns, and how his customers reacted to the deep crisis at hand. He merely connected the dots. His proposed program included relief for the unemployed, government spending on public works, government refinancing of mortgages, a federal minimum wage, federally supported old-age pensions, and higher income taxes and inheritance taxes on the wealthy in order to control capital accumulations and avoid excessive speculation. Not until these recommendations were implemented, Eccles warned, could the economy be fully restored.

Eccles then returned to Utah, from where he watched Roosevelt hatch the first hundred days of his presidency. To Eccles, the new president's initiatives seemed barely distinguishable from what his predecessor, Herbert Hoover, had offered—a hodgepodge of ideas cooked up by Wall Street to keep it afloat but do little for anyone else. "New York, as usual, seems to be in the saddle, dominating fiscal and monetary policy," he wrote to his friend George Dern, the former governor of Utah who had become Roosevelt's secretary of war.

In mid-December 1933, Eccles received a telegram from Roosevelt's Treasury secretary, Henry Morgenthau, Jr., asking him to return to Washington at the earliest possible date to "talk about monetary matters." Eccles was perplexed. The new administration had shown no interest in his ideas. He had never met Morgenthau, who was a strong advocate for balancing the federal budget. After their meeting, the mystery only deepened. Morgenthau asked Eccles to write a report on monetary policy, which

Eccles could as easily have written in Utah. A few days later Morgenthau invited Eccles to his home, where he asked about Eccles's business connections, his personal finances, and the condition of his businesses, namely whether any had gone bankrupt. Finally, Morgenthau took Eccles into his confidence. "You've been recommended as someone I should get to help me in the Treasury Department," Morgenthau said. Eccles was taken aback, and asked for a few days to think about it.

"'Here you are, Marriner, full of talk about what the government should and shouldn't do,'" Eccles told himself, as he later recounted in his memoirs. "'You ought to put up or shut up. . . . You're afraid your theory won't work. You're afraid you'll be a damned fool. You want to stick it out in Utah and wear the hair shirt of a prophet crying in the wilderness. You can feel noble that way, and you run no risks. [But] if you don't come here you'll probably regret it for the rest of your life.'" Eccles talked himself into the job.

For many months thereafter, Eccles steeped himself in the work of the Treasury and the Roosevelt administration, pushing his case for why the government needed to go deeper into debt to prop up the economy, and what it needed to do for average people. Apparently he made progress. Roosevelt's budget of 1934 contained many of Eccles's ideas, violating the president's previous promise to balance the federal budget. The president "swallowed the violation with considerable difficulty," Eccles wrote.

The following summer, after the governor of the Federal Reserve Board unexpectedly resigned, Morgenthau recommended Eccles for the job. Eccles had not thought about the Fed as a vehicle for advancing his ideas. But a few weeks later, when the president summoned him to the White House to ask if he'd be interested, Eccles told Roosevelt he'd take the job if the Federal Reserve in Washington had more power over the supply of money, and the New York Fed (dominated by Wall Street bankers) less. Eccles knew Wall Street wanted a tight money supply and correspondingly high interest rates, but the Main Streets of America— the real economy—needed a loose money supply and low rates. Roosevelt agreed to support new legislation that would tip the scales toward Main Street. Eccles took over the Fed.

For the next fourteen years, with great vigor and continuing vigilance for the welfare of average people, Eccles helped steer the economy through the remainder of the Depression and through World War II. He would also become one of the architects of the Great Prosperity that the nation and much of the rest of the world enjoyed after the war.

Eccles retired to Utah in 1950 to write his memoirs and reflect on what had caused the largest economic trauma ever to have gripped America, the Great Depression. Its major cause, he concluded, had nothing whatever to do with excessive spending during the 1920s. It was, rather, the vast accumulation of income in the hands of the wealthiest people in the nation, which siphoned purchasing power away from most of the rest. This was Eccles's biggest and most important insight. It has direct bearing on the Great Recession that started at the end of 2007. In Eccles's words:

> As mass production has to be accompanied by mass consumption, mass consumption, in turn, implies a distribution of wealth—not of existing wealth, but of wealth as it is currently produced—to provide men with buying power equal to the amount of goods and services offered by the nation's economic machinery. Instead of achieving that kind of distribution, a giant suction pump had by 1929–1930 drawn into a few hands an increasing portion of currently

produced wealth. This served them as capital accumulations. But by taking purchasing power out of the hands of mass consumers, the savers denied to themselves the kind of effective demand for their products that would justify a reinvestment of their capital accumulations in new plants. In consequence, as in a poker game where the chips were concentrated in fewer and fewer hands, the other fellows could stay in the game only by borrowing. When their credit ran out, the game stopped.

The borrowing had taken the form of mortgage debt on homes and commercial buildings, consumer installment debt, and foreign debt. Eccles understood that this debt bubble was bound to burst. And when it did, consumer spending would shrink.

And so it did. When there were no more poker chips to be loaned on credit, debtors were forced to curtail their consumption. This naturally reduced the demand for goods of all kinds and brought on higher unemployment. Unemployment further decreased the consumption of goods, which further increased unemployment.

For Eccles, widening inequality was the main culprit.

2

Parallels

If Eccles's insight into the major cause of the Great Depression sounds familiar to you, that's no coincidence. Although the Depression was far more severe than the Great Recession that officially began in December 2007, the two episodes are closely related. As Mark Twain once observed, history does not repeat itself, but it sometimes rhymes. Had America not experienced the Great Depression, policymakers eighty years later would not have learned how to use fiscal and monetary policies to contain the immediate economic threat posed by the Great Recession. But we did not learn the *larger* lesson of the 1930s: that when the distribution of income gets too far out of whack, the economy needs to be reorganized so the broad middle class has enough buying power to rejuvenate the economy over the longer term. Until we take this lesson to heart, we will be living with the Great Recession's aftershock of high unemployment and low wages, and an increasingly angry middle class.

The wages of the typical American hardly increased in the three decades leading up to the Crash of 2008, considering inflation. In the 2000s, they actually dropped. According to the Census Bureau, in 2007 a male worker earning the median male wage (that is, smack in the middle, with as many men earning more than he did as earning less) took home just over $45,000. Considering inflation, this was *less* than the typical male worker earned thirty years before. Middle-class family incomes were only slightly higher.*

But the American economy was much larger in 2007 than it was thirty years before. If those gains had been divided equally among Americans, the typical person would be more than 60 percent better off than he actually was by 2007. Where did the gains go? As in the years preceding the Great Depression, a growing share went to the top. It was just like Eccles's "giant suction pump," drawing "into a few hands an increasing portion" of the nation's total earnings.

Economists Emmanuel Saez and Thomas Piketty have exam-

---

*There is no strict definition of the "middle class." For the purposes of simplicity and clarity, I define it broadly to include the 40 percent of American families with incomes above the median family income and the 40 percent below.

ined tax records extending back to 1913. They discovered an interesting pattern. The share of total income going to the richest 1 percent of Americans peaked in both 1928 and in 2007, at over 23 percent (see Figure 1, facing page). The same pattern held for the richest one-tenth of 1 percent (representing about 150,000 households in 2007): Their share of total income also peaked in 1928 and 2007, at over 11 percent. And the same pattern applies for the richest 10 percent, who in each of these peak years received almost half the total.

Between the two peaks is a long, deep valley. After 1928, the share of national income going to the top 1 percent steadily declined, from more than 23 percent to 16–17 percent in the 1930s, then to 11–15 percent in the 1940s, and to 9–11 percent in the 1950s and 1960s, finally reaching the valley floor of 8–9 percent in the 1970s. After this, the share going to the richest 1 percent began to climb again: 10–14 percent of national income in the 1980s, 15–19 percent in the late 1990s, and over 21 percent in 2005, reaching its next peak of more than 23 percent in 2007. (At this writing, there are no data after 2007.) If you look at the shares going to the top 10 percent, or even the top one-tenth of 1 percent, you'll see the same long valley in between the two peaks.

In the 1920s, when Marriner Eccles was still a banker in Utah, it looked as if American capitalism was splitting by class. Sociologists Robert S. Lynd and his wife, Helen Merrell Lynd, after observing life in Muncie, Indiana (then a small city of thirty-five thousand that the Lynds took to be representative of America and which they called "Middletown"), recorded the growing division:

> At first glance it is difficult to see any semblance of pattern in the workaday life of a community exhibiting a crazy-quilt array of nearly four hundred ways of getting its living.... On closer scrutiny, however, this welter may be resolved into two kinds of activities. The people who engage in them will be

FIGURE I

Top 1 Percent Share of Total Income

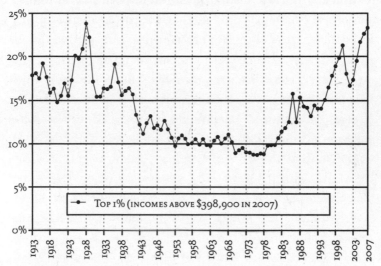

Source: Thomas Piketty and Emmanuel Saez, "The Evolution of Top Incomes: A Historical and International Perspective"

referred to throughout this report as the Working Class and the Business Class. Members of the first group, by and large, address their activities in getting their living primarily to things, utilizing material tools in the making of things and the performance of services, while the members of the second group address their activities predominantly to people in the selling or promotion of things, services, and ideas. . . . There are two and one-half times as many in the working class as in the business class. . . . It is after all this division into working class and business class that constitutes the outstanding cleavage in Middletown. The mere fact of being born upon one or the other side of the watershed roughly formed by these two groups is the most significant single cultural factor tending to influence what one does all day long throughout one's life.

By 2007, America's "working class" was making fewer "things" and offering more personal services, but the gap between them and the executives at the top had grown as large as it was in the 1920s. Muncie, Indiana, had more than doubled in size, yet the big manufacturers that once provided jobs to Muncie's working class—Delco Remy, Westinghouse, Indiana Steel and Wire, General Motors, and BorgWarner—had closed in the 1980s and 1990s. By 2007, Muncie's largest employers were Wal-Mart, Ball Memorial Hospital and Cardinal Health System, Ball State University, Muncie Community Schools, the quasi-government financial corporation Sallie Mae, and the City of Muncie. Meanwhile, Muncie's (and America's) old "business class" had become smaller, better educated, and more professional—increasingly centered in the executive suites of large corporations and financial firms. The two groups—working class and business class— once again earned vastly different wages and benefits and had sharply different ways of life.

Across the nation, the most affluent Americans have been seceding from the rest of the nation into their own separate geographical communities with tax bases (or fees) that can underwrite much higher levels of services. They have moved into office parks and gated communities, and relied increasingly on private security guards instead of public police, private spas and clubs rather than public parks and pools, and private schools (or elite public ones in their own upscale communities) for their children rather than the public schools most other children attend. Being rich now means having enough money that you don't have to encounter anyone who isn't. The middle class and the poor, meanwhile, rely on public services whose funding is ever more precarious: schools whose classrooms are more crowded; public parks and libraries open fewer hours and often less attended to; and buses and subways that are more congested. The adjective "public" in public services has often come to mean "inadequate."

There is another parallel. In the years leading up to 2007, with the real wages of the middle class flat or dropping, the only way they could keep on buying—raising their living standards in proportion to the nation's growing output—was by going deep into debt. "As in a poker game where the chips were concentrated in fewer and fewer hands, the other fellows could stay in the game only by borrowing," as Eccles put it. Savings had averaged 9–10 percent of after-tax income from the 1950s to the early 1980s, but by the mid-2000s were down to just 3 percent. The drop in savings had its mirror image in household debt (including mortgages), which rose from 55 percent of household income in the 1960s to an unsustainable 138 percent by 2007. Ominously, much of this debt was backed by the rising market value of people's homes.

The years leading up to the Great Depression saw a similar pattern. Between 1913 and 1928, the ratio of private credit to the total national economy nearly doubled. Total mortgage debt was almost three times higher in 1929 than in 1920. Eventually, in 1929, as in 2008, there were "no more poker chips to be loaned on credit," in Eccles's words. And "when . . . credit ran out, the game stopped."

A third parallel: In both periods, richer Americans used their soaring incomes and access to credit to speculate in a limited range of assets. With so many dollars pursuing the same assets, values exploded. The Dow Jones Industrial Average reached eight thousand on July 16, 1997, and eleven thousand on May 3, 1999.

More money poured into dot-coms than could be efficiently used, then into more miles of fiber-optic cable than could ever be profitable. The Dow dropped when these bubbles burst but recovered on self-fulfilling expectations of even higher share prices to come—rising to twelve thousand on October 19, 2006, then to thirteen thousand on April 25, 2007. With easy access to credit, the middle class joined in the party, boosting housing prices to all-time highs. Yet it is an iron law of economics, as well as of physics, that expanding bubbles eventually burst.

In the 1920s, richer Americans created stock and real estate bubbles that foreshadowed those of the late 1990s and 2000s. The Dow Jones Stock Index ballooned from 63.9 in mid-1921 to a peak of 381.2 eight years later, before it plunged. There was also frantic speculation in land. The Florida real estate boom lured thousands of investors into the Everglades, from where many never returned, at least financially.

Wall Street cheered them on in the 1920s, making a ton of money off gullible investors, almost exactly as it would in the 2000s. In 1928, Goldman Sachs and Company created the Goldman Sachs Trading Corporation, which promptly went on a speculative binge, luring innocent investors along the way. Four years later, after the giant bubble burst, Mr. Sachs appeared before the Senate.

SENATOR COUZENS [*Republican from Michigan*]: Did Goldman, Sachs and Company organize the Goldman Sachs Trading Corporation?

MR. SACHS: Yes, sir.

SENATOR COUZENS: And it sold its stock to the public?

MR. SACHS: A portion of it. The firm invested originally in 10 percent of the entire issue. . . .

SENATOR COUZENS: And the other 90 percent was sold to the public?

MR. SACHS: Yes, sir.

SENATOR COUZENS: At what price?

MR. SACHS: At 104 . . .

SENATOR COUZENS: And at what price is the stock now?

MR. SACHS: Approximately 1¾.

Meanwhile, National City Bank, which eventually would become Citigroup, repackaged bad Latin American debt as new securities, which it then sold to investors no less gullible than Goldman Sachs's. After the Crash, National City's top executives helped themselves to the bank's remaining assets as interest-free loans, while their investors and depositors were left with pieces of paper worth a tiny fraction of what they had paid for them.

Yet however much Wall Street's daredevil antics in the 1920s and in the 2000s were proximate causes of the giant bubbles of these two eras, the bubbles also reflected the deeper problems Eccles identified—the growing imbalance between what most people earned as workers and what they spent as consumers, and the increasingly lopsided share of total income going to the top. In both eras, had the share going to the middle class not fallen, middle-class consumers would not have needed to go as deeply into debt in order to sustain their middle-class lifestyle. Had the rich received a smaller share, they would not have bid up the prices of speculative assets so high.

The biggest difference between the two eras was in what happened *next,* after the bubbles burst. In the wake of the Great Crash of 1929, the economy went into a vicious downward cycle. Unemployed workers, with little or no access to credit, were unable to purchase much of anything. This caused businesses to lay off even more workers, which further contracted spending, leading to even more layoffs. The resulting Great Depression shook America to its core. The magnitude of that crisis forced the nation to seek ways to overcome both the widening economic divide that had contributed to it and the economic insecurities it fueled. The undeniable reality that almost all Americans shared the ravages of the Depression resulted in an unusual degree of social cohesion, giving the nation the political will to make the needed reforms.

Government policies in the wake of the Great Depression led to a new economic order, including many of the programs Marriner Eccles proposed on the eve of Roosevelt's inauguration—social insurance, and improvements in the nation's infrastructure, schools, and public universities. Initially, these were financed by government borrowing. They made the American middle class in subsequent years vastly more secure, prosperous, and productive. As we shall examine in more detail, unemployment insurance, Social Security in old age, disability benefits, and, eventually, Medicare and Medicaid propped up incomes even when misfortune struck. After World War II, a vast expansion of public higher education, interstate highways, and defense-sponsored research and development of sophisticated technologies improved workers' productivity and wages. And support of their rights to form labor unions, work at a base of forty hours and get time and a half overtime, and receive a minimum wage improved their bargaining power. During the war, government spending reached unprecedented levels. The nation put its full industrial capacity to use, employing almost all working-age Americans. And even though that capacity was largely dedicated to military demands, the sheer volume of production also met civilian needs. By the end of the war, most surviving Americans were better off than they had been at its start, and the Great Depression had irrevocably ended. America's debt was huge, to be sure, but in subsequent years a buoyant economy enabled government to repay a substantial portion.

The Great Recession that started at the end of 2007, however, has produced no new economic order. Instead, the government stepped in quickly with enough money to contain the downward slide. America had at least learned the superficial lesson Marriner Eccles had offered to deal with downdrafts of this magnitude: When demand evaporates, government must act as purchaser of last resort, temporarily filling much of the vacuum created by fast-retreating consumers, and it must make borrowing so cheap as to keep banks solvent and credit moderately available. Between 2008 and 2010, the Obama administration and the Federal Reserve played their parts with $700 billion in bank bailouts, a subsequent stimulus package of similar magnitude, and a massive expansion of the money supply.

The government thereby averted what in all likelihood would have become another Great Depression. No rational person could wish for a repeat of that. Yet, ironically, President Obama's success in forestalling economic collapse reduced the urgency of dealing with the larger challenge. Apart from extending health insurance coverage, little was done to reduce the underlying, cumulative problem of widening inequality—Eccles's insight into what caused the Great Depression. After the stimulus and loose money wear off, therefore, it is unlikely that growth can be sustained. We are almost certainly in store for many years of high unemployment. The underlying trend of the last thirty years will continue: Median incomes will remain flat or decline, and most families will stay economically insecure. Inequality will continue to widen. Consequently, the middle class will not be able to buy nearly enough to keep the economy going. Neither richer Americans nor foreign consumers will fill the gap. All of this will constitute the Great Recession's aftershock. From it will emerge either a political backlash—against trade, immigration, foreign investment, big business, Wall Street, and government itself—or large-scale reforms that reverse the underlying trend.

3

The Basic Bargain

On January 5, 1914, Henry Ford announced that he was paying workers on his famously productive Model T assembly line in Highland Park, Michigan, $5 per eight-hour day. That was almost three times what the typical factory employee earned at the time. In light of this audacious move, some lauded Ford as a friend of the American worker; others called him a madman or a socialist, or both. *The Wall Street Journal* termed his action "an economic crime." Ford thought it a cunning business move, and history proved him right. The higher wage turned Ford's autoworkers into customers who eventually could afford to plunk down $575 for a Model T. Their purchases in effect returned some of those $5 paychecks to Ford, and helped finance even higher productivity in the future. Ford was neither a madman nor a socialist, but a smart capitalist whose profits more than doubled from $25 million in 1914 to $57 million two years later.

Ford understood the basic economic bargain that lay at the heart of a modern, highly productive economy. Workers are also consumers. Their earnings are continuously recycled to buy the goods and services other workers produce. But if earnings are inadequate and this basic bargain is broken, an economy produces more goods and services than its people are capable of purchasing. This can lead to the vicious cycle Marriner Eccles witnessed after the Great Crash of 1929 and that the United States began to experience in 2008. (Global trade complicates this bargain but doesn't negate it, as I will discuss later.)

In his time, Ford's philosophy was the exception. From the 1870s to the 1930s, during what might be termed the first stage of modern American capitalism, most workers didn't share in the bounty. Large factories, mammoth machinery, and a raft of new inventions (typewriters, telephones, electric lightbulbs, aluminum, vulcanized rubber, to name just a few) dramatically increased productivity. But most working people earned far less than five dollars a day. America's burgeoning income and wealth was concentrated in fewer hands. Consequently, demand couldn't possibly keep up. Periodic busts ensued. The wholesale price index, which had stood at 193 in 1864, fell to 82 by 1890. Sharp downturns continued to jolt the economy. By the first decades of the twentieth century, the economy had stabilized, but productivity gains continued to outpace most Americans' earnings. The rich, meanwhile, used their increasing fortunes to speculate—making the economy more susceptible to cycles of boom and bust. Eccles saw this pattern eventually culminate in the Great Depression.

British economist John Maynard Keynes also understood the crucial connection between the level of wages and the demand for what workers produced. A tall, charming, self-confident Cambridge don, Keynes was born in Cambridge, England, in 1883, the same year Karl Marx died. Yet his writings probably saved capitalism from itself and surely kept latter-day Marxists at bay. During the depths of the Great Depression, when many doubted capitalism would survive, Keynes declared capitalism the best system ever devised to achieve a civilized economic society. But he recognized in it two major faults—"its failure to provide for full employment and its arbitrary and inequitable distribution of wealth and incomes." Until these were corrected, Keynes argued, capitalism would continue to be highly unstable, vulnerable to economic booms that would often be followed by catastrophic collapses. Yet if government worked to correct these faults, he felt confident that future generations could inherit a stable and prosperous world.

Classical economists had viewed markets as self-correcting. They had supposed that full employment would always prevail in the end. Any spate of unemployment would cause wages to drop until employers found it profitable to hire workers again. By this view, persistent unemployment was the result of stubborn resistance on the part of workers who insisted on keeping their old level of wages even though they didn't work hard enough to justify them. The only answer was to make them experience joblessness long enough to accept lower wages. This view fit nicely into the prevailing Social Darwinism of the era: Only the fittest should survive, and any effort to make the less fit more comfortable was bound to inflict harm on the greater society. After the Great Crash of 1929, Herbert Hoover's secretary of the Treasury, millionaire industrialist Andrew Mellon, reflecting this prevailing view, cautioned against government action. He advised that wages and prices should be allowed to fall, thereby clearing the system of waste and lassitude. "Liquidate labor, liquidate stocks, liquidate the farmer, liquidate real estate. It will purge the rottenness out of the system. . . . People will work harder, lead a more moral life." This was the same nonsense Marriner Eccles had come up against, leading Eccles to conclude that people in power were trying to justify the status quo by invoking a dubious morality.

Like Eccles, Keynes did not view unemployment as a moral failing. He saw it as a failure of demand. Average workers lacked enough purchasing power to buy what they produced. Keynes's big idea was to use macroeconomic policy to maintain full employment. Policymakers should expand the money supply to permanently lower interest rates, so that consumers and businesses could get lower-cost loans, and government should increase its own spending to make up for the shortfall in consumer demand, so that more jobs would be created.

Part of Keynes's answer was also to spread the benefits of economic growth. Keynes recognized that growth depends on the incentives of the rich to save and invest. But he noted that until an economy reaches full employment, additional savings don't help; in fact, they cause harm by reducing the demand for goods and services. The central problem isn't too little savings; it's too little demand for all the goods and services an economy can produce. This logic led Keynes to conclude that "measures for the redistribution of incomes in a way likely to raise the propensity to consume may prove positively favorable to the growth of capital."

Keynes thereby offered a theoretical explanation and a practical justification for doing what Marriner Eccles thought government should do under the conditions Eccles witnessed: maintain aggregate demand so that the productive capacity of an economy doesn't outrun the ability of ordinary people to buy, which would give businesses less incentive to invest. Equally important, enforce a basic bargain giving workers a proportionate share of the fruits of economic growth. The two went hand in glove. When the basic bargain is maintained, the entire economy is balanced. When the basic bargain breaks down, government must step in to reinforce it, or the economy will shrink.

America learned this lesson in the Great Depression. We also learned it in the Great Prosperity that followed. After that, we forgot it. Now and in years to come we must remember it.

4

How Concentrated Income at the Top Hurts the Economy

The economic problem Eccles identified and Keynes formalized arises not because the rich live too well relative to everyone else but, paradoxically, because they live too modestly—at least compared to what they can afford. When income is concentrated in relatively few hands, the overall demand for goods and services shrinks because the very rich do not nearly spend everything they earn. Their savings are hoarded, circulated in a fury of speculation, or, especially these days, invested abroad. Some savings find their ways into new domestic investment, but, as Eccles observed, usually only "when the purchasing power of the masses increases their demands for a higher standard of living." Without adequate consumer demand, investors won't foresee enough return to make the investments worthwhile.

Rich Americans may sometimes be conspicuous consumers, but overall they simply do not spend enough. Warren Buffett is an extreme example. The richest man in the world in 2008, with a net worth estimated to be $62 billion, Buffett called money "little pieces of paper that I can turn into consumption." But to a remarkable extent he chose not to consume. In 2008 he still lived on Farnam Street in the central Dundee neighborhood of Omaha, Nebraska, in the same gray stucco house he bought in 1958 for $31,500. His children attended public schools and shared the family car when they were old enough to drive. He paid for his grandchildren's college tuition but gave them nothing more. Buffet's one indulgence was a Gulfstream IV-SP jet that cost $10 million, which he sheepishly named *The Indefensible*.

Buffett's parsimony might be considered admirable, but, paradoxically, it contributed to the larger economic problem. "If I wanted to," Buffett once said, "I could hire ten thousand people to do nothing but paint my picture every day for the rest of my life. And the [gross national product] would go up. But the utility of the product would be zilch, and I would be keeping those ten thousand people from doing AIDS research, or teaching, or nursing. I don't do that, though. . . . There's nothing material I want very much." Buffett's economic logic missed a significant fact that John Maynard Keynes emphasized: Every dollar that's actually spent in an economy has a multiplier effect. Not only does it go to the person who first receives it, but also, indirectly, to other people whom the recipient of the original dollar pays for the things *he* needs. They, in turn, buy from others. Had Buffett spent more of his income, he would have sustained more jobs. Each of the ten thousand people he hired to paint his portrait would spend the money he paid them, thereby generating employment and income for many others. All of them, painters included, would also pay taxes. And their spending and tax payments might well support, directly or indirectly, AIDS research, teaching, nursing, and other endeavors more socially useful than the ten thousand portraits of Warren Buffett.

Consider the nearly $100 million Kenneth Lewis earned as CEO of Bank of America in 2007, as he was leading the bank toward a subsequent bailout by the federal government. To spend it all, Lewis would have had to buy $273,972.60 worth of goods and services every day that year, including weekends. If he had devoted twelve waking hours a day to the task, he'd have had to spend $22,831 every hour, $380.52 every minute.

In the year prior to Lehman Brothers' catastrophic inability to pay its bills, its then CEO, Richard Fuld, collected $500 million of compensation in salary and shares of stock. Fuld had a penthouse on Park Avenue then valued at $21 million; an estate in Greenwich, Connecticut, worth an estimated $25 million; and an art collection valued at $200 million. Steve Schwarzman, head of the private equity firm the Blackstone Group, was another free spender. He held a sixtieth birthday party for himself that cost $5 million. Paul Allen, cofounder of Microsoft, owned two 757s and a helicopter. But these and other high rollers—the modern equivalents of the Vanderbilts, the Carnegies, and the Rockefellers, who built mansions, threw grand parties, and owned their own railroads and oil wells in the late nineteenth and early twentieth centuries—still manage to spend only a modest portion of their yearly incomes.

It is a problem few of us are acquainted with, but the fact is that the richest human beings find it difficult to spend more than a fraction of their fortunes, notwithstanding an abundance of pricey temptations. The sheer magnitude of the task of spending obscene amounts of money can be surprisingly challenging. Few people have the time, energy, or stamina that's required. The true advantage of a fortune lies less in its purchasing power than in its power to confer high social standing and attract the adoring and enthusiastic attention of other people who want some of it.

Nor, it turns out, do most rich people have the appetite to spend all the money they accumulate. Being rich changes the very nature of desire. As we shall examine in more detail later, happiness diminishes rapidly after the first flush of acquisitive excitement. That second piece of pie never tastes quite as good as the first. Once we have had our fill of anything, additional portions aren't as attractive to us. (In some cases they can even make us sick.) How much additional bliss can one obtain from owning a fourth home or a fifth sports car or from sitting down, for the hundredth time, to a dinner of $80-an-ounce Beluga caviar and Corton-Charlemagne wine? Paul Allen's first 757 jet may have lifted his spirits as well as his body, but it's doubtful he experiences the same rush from having two.

One ethical argument for redistributing income from rich to poor comes from this psychological truth. The nineteenth-century founder of a branch of ethics called "utilitarianism," Jeremy Bentham, thought the purpose of all law should be to produce the greatest possible happiness, counting each person's happiness equally. Taking a thousand dollars from someone who's rich and giving it to someone who's poor might diminish the former's happiness slightly, Bentham reasoned, but would almost certainly increase the happiness of the poor person far more. Taxing the wealthy to help the poor, as Bentham saw it, therefore increases the sum total of happiness.

But Marriner Eccles and John Maynard Keynes saw a broader economic justification for organizing the economy in such a way that the rich did not accumulate a disproportionate share to begin with: the need to maintain enough total demand. Assume that Ken Lewis somehow managed to spend a quarter of his $100 million compensation in 2007. That would have left him with $75 million. While his $25 million of spending likely would have created lots of American jobs—construction workers who built new additions to his estates; restaurant and retail workers who catered to his appetites; doctors and hospital workers who attended to his health; financial consultants, accountants, and tax attorneys who managed his money; personal trainers, therapists, coaches, and masseurs who attended to his psychological stresses; technicians who repaired and upgraded his music systems, his personal communications systems, and his cars; people who cleaned his homes, laundered his clothing, and tended to his gardens; those who piloted his personal jets and drove his limousine—his $75 million of savings would have created far fewer. Even if invested rather than hoarded or circulated in a frenzy of speculation, the money would have moved at the speed of an electronic impulse wherever around the world it could get the highest return. (To be sure, many of the goods he bought likely would have been assembled abroad; but the largest portion of his direct spending would remain here, mostly for services.)

Now suppose Ken Lewis's $100 million had instead been divided among five hundred people, each of whom took home $200,000 that year. Assume that each spent $150,000—hardly difficult in and around New York City, or in other big cities—and saved $50,000. Total spending by those five hundred would have added up to $75 million, most of it supporting jobs in the United States. Take the logic a step further. Suppose Lewis's $100 million had been paid instead to two thousand people, each of whom took home $50,000—just about what the typical American family earned in 2007. Each of those two thousand families is likely to spend all, or nearly all, of that money. The lion's share will be for services. Most of that $100 million would have gone directly into the U.S. economy, sustaining jobs.

Before the 2008 meltdown, about half of U.S. consumer spending was done by the highest-earning fifth of the population. Roughly 40 percent of total spending came from the top 10 percent. But that was hardly because richer Americans were spendthrifts; it was because the top 10 percent took home almost 50 percent of total income. Had the broad middle class taken home a larger portion, total spending would likely have been far greater—and the middle class would not have had to go so deeply into debt.

This is not an argument for more personal consumption, per se. It is rather an argument for paying attention to total demand for all types of goods and services a society might need and be capable of producing—including, hopefully, those that conserve energy and reduce carbon emissions. Greater consumption of education, public recreation, and the arts would also, presumably, make daily life more useful and pleasant for more people without increasing *material* consumption at all.

Many of America's very rich have been exceedingly generous.

Andrew Carnegie built libraries and opera houses. John D. Rockefeller and his sons established a famously important foundation. During the most recent swing of the pendulum, Bill and Melinda Gates set up another large foundation—and in June 2006, Warren Buffett pledged a huge share of his total wealth to support its activities. These are all commendable acts, but they are beside the point I am trying to make, which is that they do not, in and of themselves, generate more jobs and more economic growth than would be the case had a larger percentage of the nation's people shared a bigger portion of the nation's bounty. (From a moral perspective, the balance here is delicate, of course. Had Microsoft been broken up and its software made generally available at lower prices, for example, middle-class Americans would have had more money to spend on, say, flat-screen TVs, while Bill Gates's correspondingly smaller fortune might have caused him to donate less to AIDS research and other Gates Foundation priorities.)

The lure of great wealth undoubtedly inspires great entrepreneurial zeal, to the benefit of all. Businesses need to be able to attract the necessary talent. The question is what portion of total national income must go to the very top in order to provide adequate motivation. On the evidence of what occurred after 2007, for example, it seems fair to conclude that Richard Fuld's $500 million compensation that year failed to provide the incentive needed for him to act in ways that benefited Lehman Brothers' shareholders and customers, and it seems doubtful that a higher sum would have produced a much better result. Indeed, it seems unlikely that he would have performed any worse had he earned just $10 million, or even a paltry $2 million. The high-stakes lure of vast sums can spur great achievement, but as Keynes observed when considering the large disparities of income and wealth in Britain in the 1920s, "much lower stakes will serve the purpose equally well."

Eccles's insight is no criticism of the rich. It points instead to a different organization of the economy and society, one that allows a broader sharing of the gains of economic growth. To this end it requires that policymakers focus on the real economy, not only the financial one.

5

Why Policymakers Obsess About the Financial Economy Instead of About the Real One

September 26, 2008. "This sucker could go down," President George W. Bush warns congressional leaders meeting with him in the White House, as he tries to wrest their agreement to a $700 billion bailout of Wall Street. A few weeks later, the most dogmatically conservative administration in recent American history—which had consistently and vociferously argued against giving anyone a helping hand for fear they'd become dependent on government—delivers the goods. "Without this rescue plan," President Bush explains to the nation, "the costs to the American economy could be disastrous." New Hampshire senator Judd Gregg, the leading Republican negotiator of the bailout bill, adds ominously, "If we do not do this, the trauma, the chaos, and the disruption to everyday Americans' lives will be overwhelming, and that's a price we can't afford to risk paying."

In less than a year, Wall Street was back. The six largest remaining banks had grown larger; their executives and traders were as rich or richer, their strategies of placing large bets with other people's money no less bold than they were before the meltdown of September 2008. The possibility of new financial regulations emanating from Congress barely inhibited the Street's exuberance. The Dow Jones Industrial Average had made up for some of its losses, and the financial recovery was proceeding nicely.

But Senator Gregg notwithstanding, the everyday lives of large numbers of Americans continued to be subject to overwhelming trauma, chaos, and disruption.

It is a common practice among economic policymakers to fervently and sincerely believe that Wall Street's financial health is not only a precondition for a prosperous real economy but that when the former thrives, the latter will necessarily follow. Few fictions of modern economic life are more assiduously defended than the central importance of the Street to the well-being of the rest of us.

Inhabitants of the real economy, including corporations and small business owners, do need to borrow money from the financial economy. But their overwhelming reliance on Wall Street is a relatively recent phenomenon. Back when middle-class Americans earned enough to be able to save more of their incomes, they borrowed from one another through intermediaries called local commercial banks and "savings and loans"—the sorts of institutions Marriner Eccles ran. Wall Street's main function was to shepherd new issues of stock. But over time, rules were loosened. The Depression-era law separating investment from commercial banking was repealed in 1999 when the Street convinced Congress (and the Clinton administration) that it had outlived its usefulness, and today the Street's major function is to make financial bets. Wall Street is a casino in which high-stakes wagers are placed within a limited number of betting houses that keep a percentage of the wins for themselves and fob off losses on others, including taxpayers.

Many economic policymakers cannot see the real economy because their formative years have been spent on Wall Street and they share its myopic view of finance as the crucial center of the economy. Presidents routinely appoint Treasury secretaries from the Street who cannot help but double as the Street's ambassador to the White House. It is easy to understand policymakers' being seduced by the great flows of wealth created by the denizens of the Street, from whom they invariably seek advice. One of the basic assumptions of capitalism is that anyone paid huge sums of money must be worth it. Policymakers are not immune to this logic. Who among us is? Besides, the culture of high finance is attractive. It promises exquisite and unimaginable levels of comfort. The limousines and private jets that transport financiers, the hushed conference rooms, the luxurious accommodations, all add to the mystique. But this has as much relevance to the everyday economy in which most Americans work as does a masquerade ball.

The costly bailout of the Street, accompanied by massive lending to banks by the Federal Reserve, was just the largest and most recent version of what has become the standard response of policymakers to financial tremors. Officials of the Treasury and the Federal Reserve instinctively throw money in the direction of whatever assets are threatened. They talk solemnly of the importance of "stabilizing" the system and "recapitalizing" it. Roughly translated, this means saving the assets—and the asses— of bankers. We were told in 1994 that Mexico's "peso crisis" required financial rescue; in 1997, that East Asia's crisis demanded capital infusions; in 1998, that Long-Term Capital Management had to be bailed out; that after the dot-com crash and the financial anxieties set off by Enron's majestic plunge, capital markets needed additional coddling. Financial officials viewed all these rescues (Lehman Brothers' death notwithstanding) as necessary and regrettable exceptions to the heroic assumption that rational, privately interested investors are never threatened by financial crises because they are smart enough to effectively evaluate all relevant information and properly weigh all risks beforehand.

The biggest banks and a very large insurer that backed them up (AIG) were bailed out in 2008. But as the real economy on Main Streets steadily worsened, policymakers looked the other way. Officials preferred to view the meltdown as the consequence of excessively risky lending rather than the culmination of ever greater borrowing by millions of Americans who had no other way to maintain what they considered a decent living standard. To be sure, the financial economy had gone on a binge. The relative calm of preceding decades, conveniently punctuated by financial bailouts, had lured investors into taking ever greater risks, with the expectations of ever larger returns. But the locus of the problem was not in the financial economy; it was in the real economy.

When policymakers viewed the debt load taken on by ordinary Americans, they saw it as a problem to be remedied; they did not examine carefully the circumstances that caused the borrowing. Officials assumed that Americans had splurged—saving too little and buying more than they could afford. China, it was assumed, had saved too much and consumed too little, while we had done the reverse.

To be sure, in the years leading up to the Great Recession, China accumulated a substantial amount of savings and lent a big portion to the United States, from which China could secure a good return. Savings also flowed to the United States from Japan, Germany, and oil-producing nations. These savings undoubtedly made it easier for Americans to afford the costs of borrowing. But to conclude from this that the long-term answer to the nation's economic ills is for typical Americans to borrow less, save more, tighten their belts, and spend "within our means," entails a giant and questionable leap of economic logic.

Had most Americans' share of the economy's gains kept up, they could have afforded a lifestyle as good as if not better than they had before. They would have been able to save for rainy days, meeting their expenses even if they lost their jobs or their wages dipped. Consequently, they would not have felt the need to borrow as much. The problem was not that they had been living beyond their means but that their earnings had not kept up with their reasonable expectations for what they could afford as the economy grew.

The problem, in short, was that the basic bargain had been broken.

6

The Great Prosperity: 1947–1975

One of my earliest memories is the day my father brought home a TV—a large, square box with a tiny, round tube on the front, which, when switched on, would pick up shadowy shapes and voices from somewhere beyond. We weren't rich by a long shot, but my father had returned from the war with enough money to rent a store and fill it with women's cotton blouses and skirts. Factories were humming. Workers had paychecks, and the blouses and skirts sold. And with some of the profits my father bought our TV. We were the first family on the block to have one, and I remember neighbors crowding around it to watch Milton Berle in *Texaco Star Theater*. Within the decade, almost every family had its own TV.

Call it the Great Prosperity—the three decades from about 1947 to 1975. During this era, America as a whole implemented the basic bargain. The nation provided its workers enough money to buy what they produced. Mass production and mass consumption proved perfect complements. Almost everyone who wanted a job could find one with good wages, or at least wages that were trending upward. During this quarter century, everyone's wages grew—not just those in the top 1 percent, or the top 10 percent.

Go back to Figure 1 (page 21) and that long valley between the peaks and you'll see during these years a time of widely shared prosperity. The wages of lower-income Americans grew faster than those at or near the top. The pay of workers in the bottom fifth more than doubled over these years—a faster pace than the pay of those in the top fifth. By the late 1940s, the nation was "more than halfway to perfect equality," as the National Bureau of Economic Research dryly observed.

Productivity also grew quickly during these years, defying the self-serving predictions of those who said wide inequality was necessary for rapid growth because top executives and innovators needed the incentive of outsized earnings. Labor productivity—average output per hour worked—doubled, as did median incomes. Expressed in 2007 dollars, the typical family's annual income rose from about $25,000 to $55,000. The bargain was cinched.

So how did we go from the Great Depression to a quarter century of Great Prosperity? And from there, to thirty years of stagnant incomes and widening inequality, culminating in the Great Recession? It was no accident.

It is still possible to find people who believe that government policy did not end the Great Depression and undergird the Great Prosperity, just as it is possible to uncover people who do not believe in evolution. To be sure, the U.S. government refrained from doing what many of Europe's social democratic countries did—directly redistribute income from the rich to the poor and middle class, and nationalize industries. Nonetheless, it actively created the *conditions* for the middle class to fully share in the nation's prosperity. It did so by pushing the economy toward full employment, creating a more progressive income tax, enhancing the bargaining power of average workers, building up Social Security, providing workers with a strong safety net when they couldn't work, and improving their productivity.

Franklin D. Roosevelt never fully understood Keynesian economics, despite the efforts of Marriner Eccles and others to educate him, but FDR proved the success of Keynesianism. He proved it not so much by the relatively tempered government spending of the New Deal but by the astonishingly huge spending demanded by World War II. By the end of the war, when the national debt equaled almost 120 percent of the entire economy, most Americans who survived were better off than they were before the war began because they had been put to work. And although policymakers worried that the economy would thereafter slip back into depression or stagnation—"All alike expect and fear a post-war collapse," wrote economist Alvin Hansen of Harvard University—the feared collapse never came. By then the middle class—its pockets bulging with pay accumulated during the war that it was not allowed to spend during wartime—had the means to buy, and its pent-up demand for houses, cars, appliances, and almost every bit of baby paraphernalia imaginable created new jobs. And as the economy grew, the debt shrank as a percentage of it. "We're all Keynesians now," Richard Nixon purportedly proclaimed in 1971.* By then even a conservative like

---

*In fact, Nixon didn't actually say this. He said, "I am now a Keynesian in economics." The famous "We're all Keynesians now" came from a cover story in the December 31, 1965, edition of *Time* magazine, which attributed the quote to Milton Friedman. Even this wasn't precisely accurate. In a commentary appearing in the February 4, 1966, edition of *Time,* Friedman clarified that he had actually said, "In one sense we are all Keynesians now, in another, nobody any longer is a Keynesian."

Nixon had accepted government's ability to keep people employed, to fill the breach when consumers and businesses did not spend enough.

The Great Prosperity also marked the culmination of a reorganization of work that had begun during the Depression. Employers were required by law to provide extra pay—time and a half—for work stretching beyond forty hours a week. This created an incentive for employers to hire additional workers when demand picked up. Employers also were required to pay a minimum wage, which improved the pay of workers near the bottom as demand grew and employers needed more lower-skilled workers. When workers were laid off, generally during an economic downturn, government provided them with unemployment benefits, usually lasting until the economy recovered and they were rehired. Not only did this tide families over but it kept them buying goods and services—an "automatic stabilizer" for the economy in downturns. (With its anti-union "open shops" and its abundance of farm and domestic workers unprotected by labor laws, much of the South continued to lag behind, however.)

Perhaps most significantly, government increased the bargaining leverage of ordinary workers. They were guaranteed the right to join labor unions, with which employers had to bargain in good faith. By the mid-1950s, almost a third of all workers were unionized. And the unions demanded a fair slice of the American pie. United Auto Workers president Walter Reuther, among others, explicitly invoked the basic bargain: "Unless we get a more realistic distribution of America's wealth," he threatened, "we won't get enough to keep this machine going." Employers relented, and the higher wages kept America's great economic machine going better than ever by giving average workers more money to buy what they produced. And because health and pension benefits were not taxed, big employers added ever more generous provisions.

Everyone's pay in a big company, including even that of top executives, reflected bargains struck among big business, big labor, and, indirectly, government. (Postwar, regulators still set many rates and prices, awarded valuable licenses and contracts, and also settled labor disputes.) It would have been unseemly, not to say politically unwise, for executives to take home disproportionately large pay packages. The overall result was that as corporations did better, so did all their employees.

A college sociology textbook of 1956 titled *The American Class Structure* noted how far America had come from the class divisions of Middletown in the 1920s, and attributed much of the change to the new organization of production. "All are employees, not owners. Their places in the system depend upon the rules of bureaucratic entry and promotion; business is coming more and more to assume the shape of the government civil service." The author went on to show how corporate bureaucracies had a leveling effect on incomes, as the bottom rungs were elevated and the top rungs constrained by civil service–like job categories. "Income is determined by functional role in the bureaucracy. The trend of income distribution has been toward a reduction in inequality. Owners have been receiving a smaller share relative to employees; professionals and clerks have been losing some of their advantages over operatives and laborers."

Americans also enjoyed security against the risks of economic life—not only unemployment benefits but also, through Social Security, insurance against disability, loss of a major breadwinner, workplace injury, and inability to save enough for retirement. In 1965 came health insurance for the elderly and the poor (Medicare and Medicaid). Poverty among the elderly dropped by half. Economic security proved the handmaiden of prosperity. In requiring Americans to share the costs of adversity, it enabled them to share the benefits of peace of mind. Peace of mind and security freed them to consume more of the fruits of their labors.

The government sponsored the dreams of American families to own their own home by providing low-cost mortgages and interest deductions on mortgage payments. In many sections of the country, government subsidized electricity and water to make such homes affordable. And it built the roads and freeways that connected the homes with major commercial centers. The interstate highway system—forty-one thousand miles of straight four-lane (sometimes even six-lane) freeways to replace the old two-lane federal roads that meandered through cities and towns— became the single most ambitious public works program in American history. Begun under President Dwight Eisenhower and justified in the halls of Congress as a means of speeding troops, tanks, and munitions across the nation in the event of war, it did much more than that—generating sprawling suburbs and shopping malls, boosting auto sales, vastly enlarging the construction industry, creating an enormously extended trucking industry, and radically reducing the cost of transporting and distributing goods across America.

Government also widened access to higher education. The G.I. Bill paid college costs for those who returned from war. The expansion of public universities—whose tuitions averaged about 4 percent of median family income during the Great Prosperity in contrast to the 20 percent then demanded by private universities—made higher education affordable to the American middle class. Consequently, college enrollments surged. By 1970, 70 percent of the nation's four-year students were in public universities and colleges. The federal government, especially the Defense Department, also underwrote a growing portion of university research, particularly in the sciences.

Cold War defense spending generated what might be called

an "industrial commons" that spilled over into commercial production. The military-industrial complex, as Eisenhower so decorously dubbed it, invented small transistors that eventually were utilized in everything from televisions to wristwatches. The Department of Defense also researched and produced hard plastics, optical fibers, lasers, computers, jet engines and aircraft frames, precision gauges, and sensing devices. These found their way into such indispensables of modern life as graphite tennis rackets, remote-controlled television sets, microwave ovens, and cell phones. The Pentagon also gave birth to the nation's first computers. New fighter jets and engines morphed into commercial jet aircraft. Boeing's famously profitable 707 began life as the Air Force KC-135 tanker. Eventually, the Defense Advanced Research Projects Agency would give birth to the Internet.

Notwithstanding all this, the nation also found the time and the money in these years to rebuild Western Europe and Japan—spending billions of dollars to restore foreign factories, roads, railways, and schools. "The old imperialism—exploitation for foreign profit—has no place in our plans," President Harry Truman magnanimously pronounced in his Point Four program of technological assistance to developing nations. "What we envisage is a program of development based on the concept of democratic fair-dealing." (He might have added: "and the containment of the Soviet menace.") The effort proved an astounding success. The years 1945 to 1970 witnessed the most dramatic and widely shared economic growth in the history of the world, which contributed to America's Great Prosperity. In helping to restore the world's leading economies and thus keep communism at bay, the new global system of trade and assistance created vast new opportunities for American corporations—far richer, larger, and more technologically advanced than any other country's—to expand and prosper.

Government paid for all of this with tax revenues from an expanding middle class whose incomes were rising rapidly. Revenues were also boosted by those at the top of the income ladder. Income tax rates on America's top earners remained as high as if not higher than they were during World War II. The top marginal tax rate during the war ranged from 79 percent to 94 percent. In the 1950s, under President Dwight Eisenhower, whom few would call a radical, it was 91 percent. In 1964, the top rate dropped to 77 percent. It was 77 percent again in 1969, when Richard Nixon became president. Even after exploiting all possible deductions and credits, the typical high-income taxpayer during the Great Prosperity paid a federal tax of well over 50 percent of his earnings. But contrary to what conservative commentators had predicted would happen, the high tax rates did not reduce economic growth. To the contrary, they enabled the nation to expand middle-class prosperity, which fueled growth.

The Great Prosperity that lasted for a quarter century after World War II grew out of an economy profoundly different from the one that led up to the Great Depression of the 1930s. During the Great Prosperity, government enforced the basic bargain—using Keynesian policy to achieve nearly full employment, giving ordinary workers more bargaining power, providing social insurance, and expanding public investment. Consequently, the share of total income that went to the middle class grew while the portion going to the top declined. But here's the interesting thing: Because the economy expanded so buoyantly, just about everyone came out ahead—including those at the top.

Public support for government's new role had been founded in the Great Depression and World War II, in whose wake Americans shared a larger sense of common purpose. We were all in it together, rising or falling together, connected to one another in ways we had barely noticed before the Depression. None of us could prosper unless prosperity was widely shared. The historian James Truslow Adams coined the phrase "the American dream," and defined it as "a better, richer, and happier life for all our citizens of every rank."

America of that era still harbored vast inequalities, of course. The very poor remained almost invisible. Through much of the era, blacks were still relegated to second-class citizenship. Few women dared aspire to professions other than teaching or nursing. (In 1957 United Airlines proudly announced that its "executive" service between New York and Chicago featured comfortable slippers, a steak dinner, and "no women on board except for two stewardesses.") But such barriers would eventually weaken or disappear. And although the era also engendered a blandness, uniformity, and materialism that many found abhorrent—as *Mad Men,* the television drama about advertising executives in the early 1960s, demonstrates brilliantly and outrageously—the Great Prosperity offered more Americans more opportunities than ever before to make whatever life they wanted. And it proved that widely shared income gains were not incompatible with economic growth; they were, in fact, essential to it.

7

How We Got Ourselves into the Same Mess Again

As secretary of labor in the 1990s, I traveled a great deal across America. Everywhere I went I met families working harder than ever but becoming less economically secure. The pendulum was swinging back to the America Marriner Eccles had written about before the Great Depression. As I said earlier, the reversal had actually begun in the late 1970s and gathered momentum through the 1980s, 1990s, and 2000s. Middle-class wages stopped climbing even though the economy continued to expand and jobs were abundant. And almost all the benefits were again going to the top.

We in the Clinton administration tinkered. We raised the minimum wage and guaranteed workers time off from their jobs for family or medical emergencies. We tried for universal health care. We offered students from poor families access to college, and expanded a refundable tax credit for low-income workers. We tied executive compensation to company performance. All these steps were helpful but frustratingly small in light of the larger backward lunge. Federal Reserve chief Alan Greenspan—who was no Marriner Eccles—insisted that Clinton cut the federal budget deficit rather than deliver on his more ambitious campaign promises, and Greenspan reciprocated by reducing interest rates. This ushered in a strong recovery. By the late 1990s the economy was growing so quickly and unemployment was so low that middle-class wages started to rise a bit for the first time in two decades. But because the rise was propelled by an upturn in the business cycle rather than by any enduring change in the structure of the economy, it turned out to be a temporary blip. Once the economy cooled, most family incomes were barely higher than before.

During the Great Prosperity of 1947–1975, the basic bargain had ensured that the pay of American workers coincided with their output. In fact, the vast middle class received an increasing share of the benefits of economic growth. But after that point, the two lines began to diverge: Output per hour—a measure of productivity—continued to rise. But real hourly compensation was left far behind, as you can see in Figure 2 on page 52.

FIGURE 2

Growth of Average Hourly Compensation and Productivity, 1947–2008

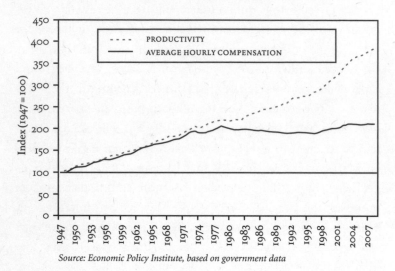

Source: *Economic Policy Institute, based on government data*

It's easy to blame "globalization" for the flattening of middle-class incomes. Yes, large numbers of American manufacturing workers began to lose their jobs in the late 1970s as factories started opening in Mexico and then in China, and by the 1990s, the jobs of even some well-trained professionals were being outsourced. But that's not the whole story. Trade also gave Americans access to cheaper goods from around the world, and it created new markets for American exports of everything from wheat to Hollywood films. Global investors also flocked to the United States to set up firms that employed millions of Americans.

The problem was not simply the loss of good jobs to workers in foreign nations but also automation. New technologies such as computerized machine tools could do the same work people did at a fraction of the cost. Even factories remaining in the United States shed workers as they automated. I remember being invited to speak at the opening ceremony of a new factory that had been lured to a midwestern state by a governor who had spent millions of taxpayer dollars subsidizing the project. When I arrived, the factory was humming at full capacity. But when I went inside to see workers performing all the new jobs, I found only about a dozen people sitting at computer terminals, typing instructions to the computerized machine tools and robots that cut, drilled, and assembled various parts into finished products. Once outside again I tried to put the best face I could on the situation. I remember stumbling over my words. "This factory marks a . . . major . . . millstone, er, milestone." I congratulated the governor and got out of there as fast as I could.

Remember bank tellers? Telephone operators? The fleets of airline workers behind counters who issued tickets? Service-station attendants? These and millions of other jobs weren't lost to globalization; they were lost to automation. America has lost at least as many jobs to automated technology as it has to trade. Any routine job that requires the same steps to be performed over and over can potentially be done anywhere in the world by someone working for far less than an American wage, *or* it can be done by automated technology. By the late 1970s, all such jobs were on the endangered species list. By 2013, they were nearly extinct.

But contrary to popular mythology, trade and technology have not really reduced the *number* of jobs available to Americans. Take a look at the rate of unemployment over the last thirty years and you'll see it has risen and fallen with the business cycle. Jobs were plentiful in the 1990s even though trade and automated technologies were pushing millions of workers out of their old jobs. The real problem was that the new ones they got often didn't pay as well as the ones they lost. That largely explains why the median wage flattened between 1980 and 2000, adjusted for inflation, and then declined between 2000 and 2013. Over the longer term, the problem is *pay*, not *jobs*. Surely for many Americans, the most traumatic consequence of the Great Recession has been the loss of a job. The good news is that more jobs will become available, eventually. The bad news is that many Americans who obtain these jobs will have to accept lower pay than they received before.

Meanwhile, as the pay of most workers has flattened or dropped, the pay of well-connected graduates of prestigious colleges and MBA programs—the so-called talent who reach the pinnacles of power in executive suites and on Wall Street—has soared.

The real puzzle is why so little was done in response to these forces that were conferring an increasing share of economic growth on a small group at the top and leaving most other Americans behind. With the gains from that growth, the nation could, for example, have expanded our educational system to encompass early-childhood education. It could have lent more support to affordable public universities, and created more job retraining and better and more extensive public transportation.

In addition, the nation could have given employees more bargaining power to get higher wages, especially in industries sheltered from global competition and requiring personal service— big-box retail stores, restaurants and hotel chains, and child and elder care, for instance. We could have enlarged safety nets to compensate for increasing anxieties about job loss: unemployment insurance covering part-time work, wage insurance if pay dropped, transition assistance to move to new jobs in new locations, insurance for entire communities that lose a major employer so they could lure other employers. We could have financed Medicare for all. Regulators could have prohibited big, profitable companies from laying off a large number of workers all at once and required them to pay severance—say, a year of wages—to anyone they let go, and train them for new jobs. The minimum wage could have been linked to inflation.

Why did we fail to raise taxes on the rich and fail to cut them for poorer Americans? Why did we fail to attack overseas tax havens by threatening loss of U.S. citizenship to anyone who keeps his money abroad in order to escape U.S. taxes? America could have expanded public investments in research and development, and required any corporation that commercialized such investments to create the resulting new jobs in the United States. And we could have insisted that foreign nations we trade with establish a minimum wage that's half their median wage. That way, all citizens could share in gains from trade, setting the stage for the creation of a new middle class that in turn could participate more fully in the global economy.

In these and many other ways, government could have enforced the basic bargain. But it did the opposite. Starting in the late 1970s, and with increasing fervor over the next three decades, it deregulated and privatized. It increased the cost of public higher education, reduced job training, cut public transportation, and allowed bridges, ports, and highways to corrode. It shredded safety nets—reducing aid to jobless families with children, and restricting those eligible for unemployment insurance so much that by 2007 only 40 percent of the unemployed were covered. It halved the top income tax rate from the range of 70 to 90 percent that prevailed during the Great Prosperity to 25 to 39 percent; allowed many of the nation's rich to treat their income as capital gains subject to no more than 15 percent tax; and shrank inheritance taxes that affected only the topmost 1.5 percent of earners. Yet at the same time, America boosted sales and payroll taxes, both of which took a bigger chunk out of the pay of the middle class and the poor than of those who were well-off.

We allowed companies to break the basic bargain with impunity—slashing jobs and wages, cutting benefits, and shifting risks to employees, from you-can-count-on-it pensions to do-it-yourself 401(k)s, from good health coverage to soaring premiums and deductibles. Companies were allowed to bust unions and threaten employees who tried to organize (by 2013, fewer than 7 percent of private-sector workers were unionized). We stood by as big American companies became global companies with no more loyalty or connection to the United States than a GPS device. By 2013, Intel, Caterpillar, Microsoft, IBM, and a raft of other so-called American firms derived most of their revenues from outside the United States, and were hiring like mad abroad.

And nothing impeded CEO salaries from skyrocketing to more than three hundred times that of the typical worker (up from thirty times during the Great Prosperity), while the pay of financial executives and traders rose into the stratosphere. Increasingly, the ranks of America's super-rich were made up of top business and financial executives. More than half of all the money that the top one-tenth of 1 percent of American earners reported on their 2001 taxes represented the combined incomes of the top *five* executives at the five hundred largest American companies. Almost all the rest were financial traders and hedge-fund managers.

Significantly, Washington deregulated Wall Street while insuring it against major losses. In so doing it turned finance—which until then had been the servant of American industry—into its master, demanding short-term profits over long-term growth, and raking in an ever-larger portion of the nation's profits. Between 1997 and 2007, finance became the fastest-growing part of the U.S. economy. The gains reaped by financial executives, traders, and specialists represented almost two-thirds of the growth in the gross national product. By 2007, financial and insurance companies accounted for more than 40 percent of American corporate profits and almost as great a percentage of pay, up from 10 percent during the Great Prosperity. Before and after the bubble burst, the biggest Wall Street banks awarded tens of billions of dollars in bonuses. In 2009, the twenty-five best-paid hedge-fund managers together earned $25.3 billion, an average of $1 billion each. Henry Ford's legacy was a company that no longer made its money exclusively from selling cars; in 2007, Ford's financial division accounted for more than a third of the company's earnings.

As the financial economy took over the real economy, Treasury and Fed officials grew in importance. The expectations of bond traders dominated public policy. And the stock market became the measure of the economy's success—just as it had before the Great Depression.

Why did the pendulum swing back? Why didn't America counteract the market forces that were shrinking the middle class's share of the American pie? Answers to these questions offer clues about when and how the pendulum will swing in the other direction.

Some argue that there was simply no need for government intervention. The economy did better on its own, those people say, without so much government and with lower taxes on the rich. They point to the great expansion of the 1980s and the long recovery of the 1990s, and to the wildly exuberant bull market of the era. (They blame the Great Recession on the fact that too many people got mortgage loans who had no business getting them, and on too much middle-class debt overall.)

This argument is bunk. It equates the stock market with the economy, and turns a blind eye to the revocation of the basic bargain. The argument does not acknowledge the consequences for an economy when the middle class lacks the means to buy what it produces.

Others see the reversal of the pendulum as the inevitable result of declining confidence in government. In their view, the era that began with the Vietnam War and continued with the Watergate scandal culminated in the tax revolts and double-digit inflation of the late 1970s—which, according to presidential candidate Ronald Reagan, occurred not because Americans were living too well but "because the government [was] living too well."

Confidence in government did drop, but proponents of this view have cause and effect backward. The tax revolts that thundered across America starting in the late 1970s were not so much ideological revolts against government—Americans still wanted all the government services they had had before, and then some— as against paying more taxes on incomes that had flattened. When government services consequently deteriorated and government deficits exploded, the public's growing cynicism was confirmed. Furthermore, the inflation of the 1970s wasn't due to government spending. It was the result of a twelvefold hike in world oil prices (engineered by the oil cartel), and a drop in value of the dollar. When inflation began to accelerate, federal spending was only one percentage point higher as a proportion of gross domestic product than it had been in the first half of the 1960s.

The real reason for the reversal of the pendulum had to do with power. As income and wealth became concentrated in fewer hands, politics reverted to what Marriner Eccles described in the 1920s when people "with great economic power had an undue influence in making the rules of the economic game." With hefty campaign contributions, and platoons of lobbyists and public relations flacks, the rich helped push through legal changes that enabled them to accumulate even more income and wealth—including tacit permission to bust unions, slash corporate payrolls, and reduce benefits; lower taxes for themselves; and deregulate Wall Street. With so much of their wealth depending on the performance of the stock market, they especially wanted to free up the Street to put greater pressure on companies to perform—for example, by making it easier for investors to mount "leveraged buyouts," pay with high-risk (junk) bonds, pump up the profits by firing workers, and then dump the company back on the market at a higher price. The plan worked. The Dow Jones Industrial Average took off, rising tenfold between 1980 and 2000. It crashed in 2008 but by 2013 had regained most of its losses and was back on track. (To be sure, the market's meteoric rise also boosted the values of middle-class pensions, which were now dependent on the stock market rather than guaranteed to pay out a certain sum each month. But the average market holdings of middle-class Americans remained tiny compared to those of wealthy Americans.)

The rich and powerful also had substantial influence "in conditioning the attitude taken by people as a whole toward [the] rules," as Eccles wrote in describing the pre-Depression years. They generously financed think tanks, books, media, and ads designed to persuade Americans that free markets always know best. Ronald Reagan, Margaret Thatcher, Alan Greenspan, Milton Friedman, and other apostles of free-market dogma reiterated a simple story: The choice was between a free market and big government. Government was the problem. Free markets were the solution.

But how could the public have been so gullible as to accept this story? After all, America had gone through a Great Depression, suffering the consequences of an unfettered market and unconstrained greed. Even Marriner Eccles, business tycoon and chairman of the Federal Reserve Board, saw that left to its own devices, the market concentrates wealth and income—which is disastrous to an economy as well as to a society. America had also experienced the Great Prosperity, which depended so obviously on public improvements, safety nets, and public investment. Now that the basic bargain was coming apart once again, the need for them was even greater.

One way to understand the paradox is loss of generational memory. While the trauma of the Great Depression echoed in the memories of people who came to adulthood in the 1930s (and who carried its lessons into the 1940s and '50s), their children became adults during the Great Prosperity, and took it for granted. And their grandchildren, born during the Great Prosperity, had no actual, palpable memory of their grandparents' experience of a fallible and unreliable market offset by a strong and reliable government. When this last generation became adults (from around the end of the 1970s onward), all they recalled was the failure of government and the apparent success of the market. This made them particularly susceptible to the seductive rants of the free marketeers, who wanted to blame government for the economy's failings. Moreover, they had no clear memory of a society whose members were all in it together. They witnessed instead an economy in which, increasingly, each of us was on his own.

8

How Americans Kept Buying Anyway: The Three Coping Mechanisms

Americans also accepted the backward swing of the pendulum because they mitigated its effects. Starting in the late 1970s, the American middle class honed three coping mechanisms, allowing it to behave as though it was still taking home the same share of total income as it had during the Great Prosperity, and to spend as if nothing substantially had changed. Not until these coping mechanisms finally became exhausted in the Great Recession would the underlying reality become evident. (And not until the federal government ended its stimulus and the Fed tightened the money supply would that reality be exposed as more enduring than the Great Recession's downturn.)

Coping mechanism #1: Women move into paid work. Starting in the late 1970s, and escalating in the 1980s and 1990s, women went into paid work in greater and greater numbers. For the relative few with four-year college degrees, this was the natural consequence of wider educational opportunities and new laws against gender discrimination that opened professions to well-educated women. But the vast majority of women who migrated into paid work did so in order to prop up family incomes, as households were hit by the stagnant or declining wages of male workers. Fortunately, the changing nature of work—from heavy manufacturing to services—opened jobs that demanded less brute strength; and the use of the contraceptive pill gave women more control over when they would have children and how many they would have, thereby allowing them to put more time and energy into making money.

This transition of women into paid work has been one of the most important social and economic changes to occur over the last four decades. It has reshaped American families and challenged traditional patterns of child rearing and child care. In 1966, 20 percent of mothers with young children worked outside the home. By the late 1990s, the proportion had risen to 60 percent. For married women with children under the age of six, the transformation has been even more dramatic—from 12 percent in the 1960s to 55 percent by the late 1990s.

Families seem to have reached the limit, however, a point of diminishing returns where the costs of hiring others to help in the running of a household or to take care of the children, or both, exceeds the apparent benefits of the additional income.

Coping mechanism #2: Everyone works longer hours. What families failed to get in wage increases, they made up for in work increases. By the mid-2000s it was not uncommon for men to work more than 50 hours a week, and for women to work more than 40. Professionals put in more "billable" hours. Hourly workers relied on overtime. A growing number of people took on two or three jobs, each demanding 20 or more hours. By the 2000s, before the Great Recession, the typical American worker put in more than 2,200 hours a year—350 hours more than the average European worked, and more hours even than the typically industrious Japanese. All told, the typical American family put in 500 additional hours of paid work, a full twelve weeks more than it had in 1979.

How did women and men work such long hours and also take care of their families, maintain their homes, pay their taxes and their bills? Not easily. Many did it in shifts. I have an acronym for such families—DINS, "double income, no sex." Here, too, though, Americans seemed to have reached a limit. Even if they could find more work, they couldn't find any more time.

Coping mechanism #3: We draw down savings and borrow to the hilt. After exhausting the first two coping mechanisms, the only way Americans could keep consuming as before was to save less and go deeper into debt. During the Great Prosperity, the American middle class saved about 9 percent of their after-tax incomes each year. By the late 1980s that portion had been whittled down to about 7 percent, and it dropped to about 6 percent in 1994. The slide continued until it reached 2.6 percent in 2008. Meanwhile, household debt exploded. During the Great Prosperity, debt had averaged 50 to 55 percent of annual after-tax income (including what people owed on their mortgages). But starting in 1980, debt took off. In 2001, Americans owed as much as their *entire* after-tax income. But the borrowing didn't even stop there, especially after the Federal Reserve Board lowered interest rates and made borrowing easier. By 2007, as I said earlier, the typical American household owed 138 percent of its after-tax income.

Americans borrowed from everywhere. Credit card solicitations flooded mailboxes; many American wallets bulged with dozens of cards, all amassing larger and larger debt loads. Auto loans were easy to come by. Students and their families went deep into debt to pay the costs of college. Mortgage debt exploded. And as housing values continued to rise, homes doubled as ATMs. Consumers refinanced their homes with even larger mortgages and used their homes as collateral for additional loans. As long as housing prices continued to rise, it seemed a painless way to get money (in 1980 the average home sold for $64,600; by 2006 it went for $246,500). Between 2002 and 2007, American households extracted $2.3 trillion from their houses, putting themselves ever more deeply into the hole.

Eventually, of course, the debt bubble burst. With it, the last coping mechanism disappeared.

It has been easy to place blame ever since. Some observers blame consumers for borrowing too much. Others fault banks for lending so carelessly. Others blame foreign lenders—especially the Chinese—who were happy to send so much money our way because we'd use some of it to buy their exports. Or they blame the Federal Reserve, which made borrowing easy by lowering interest rates too much. Or they blame regulators, who didn't adequately oversee the banks that did the lending. On it goes, a blame game much like a merry-go-round, on which every villain chases every victim, and every victim becomes a villain to another victim.

Much of this blame is justified, but it misses the point. Middle-class consumers took on the huge amount of debt as a last resort. Median wages had stopped growing, and the proportion of total income going to the middle class continued to shrink. The only way most Americans could keep consuming as if wages hadn't stalled was to run through the coping mechanisms. But each of these mechanisms reached its inevitable limit. And when the debt bubble burst, most Americans woke up to a startling reality: They could no longer afford to live as they *had* been living; nor as they thought they *should* be living relative to the lavish lifestyles of those at or near the top, nor as they *expected* to be living given their continuing aspirations for a better life, nor as they assumed they *could* be living, given the improvements they had experienced during the Great Prosperity.

9

The Future Without Coping Mechanisms

November 6, 2008. Barack Obama has just been elected president and has invited a dozen or more of us who informally advised him during the campaign to talk about the big economic challenges of the future. Paul Volcker, the former chairman of the Federal Reserve, eighty-one years old (and almost two feet taller than I am), tells the president-elect the underlying problem is that Americans have been living beyond their means. My colleague Laura Tyson, the former chair of Bill Clinton's Council of Economic Advisors, disagrees. "The real problem is their means haven't been growing."

Laura was right. The fundamental economic challenge ahead

is to lift the means of middle-class Americans and reconstitute the basic bargain linking wages to overall improvements—providing the vast American middle class with a share of economic gains sufficient to allow them to purchase more of what the economy can produce. The nation cannot achieve nearly full employment, a higher median income, and faster growth without a reorganization of the economy that spreads the benefits of growth on a scale similar to that which occurred during the Great Prosperity. It is both an economic challenge and a moral challenge; concentrated income and wealth will threaten the integrity and cohesion of our society, and will undermine democracy. But the conversation with the president-elect that fateful day in November never got this far. There was no opportunity to talk about how the increasing concentration of income and wealth had destabilized the economy. The meeting quickly shifted back to the massive debts Americans had taken on, especially mortgage debt, and from there it moved to the fragility of the nation's largest banks. This was understandable. At that moment, the immediate challenge appeared to be rescuing the financial system.

Yet until the bargain is restored, the economy will remain precarious. Some will proclaim a "recovery" on the basis of evidence that the nation has emerged from the depths of recession, but such a recovery will not be sustainable. The only positive aspect of falling into a deep hole is the absence of alternative ways of moving forward other than by climbing out. Yet none should confuse a climb out of the hole we fell into in 2008 with healthy growth over the longer term. Other holes lie ahead.

The coping mechanisms are exhausted. Now and in the foreseeable future, even if women and men were willing and able to work longer hours, there are not nearly enough jobs or hours to go around. It will be many years before the economy comes close to making up all the jobs it lost in the aftermath of the Great Recession, as well as providing jobs for all the additional people who have become available for work since the losses began. And if present trends continue, the real wages of most Americans who have, or who get, jobs will continue to erode.

The Great Recession accelerated the structural change in the economy that began in the late 1970s. More companies have found means of cutting their payrolls for good, discovering ways to use software, robots, and computer technologies to substitute for employees. Both container ships and the Internet have lowered the costs of outsourcing work to Asia and Latin America. Consequently, large numbers of Americans will not be rehired unless they are willing to settle for lower wages and fewer benefits. The official unemployment numbers hide the extent to which Americans are already on this path. Among those with jobs, more and more people have accepted lower pay and benefits as a condition for keeping them. Or they have lost higher-paying jobs and are now in new ones that pay less. Or new hires are paid far less than the old (in January 2010, Ford announced that it would add twelve hundred jobs at its Chicago assembly plant but didn't trumpet the fact that the new workers will be paid half of what current workers were paid when they began). Or they have become consultants or temporary workers whose pay is unsteady and benefits nonexistent. As I've said, over the long term, the challenge is pay, not jobs. Eventually jobs will return. But if the trend continues, more people will be working for pay they consider inadequate, and inequality will have widened.

New jobs created between the trough of the recession in 2009 and the "recovery" year of 2013 paid less, on average, than jobs that had been lost in the recession, and the Bureau of Labor statistics estimated that seven out of ten growth occupations over the next decade would be low-wage—like serving customers at big-box retailers and fast-food chains. Walmart, the nation's largest employer by 2012, paid its hourly workers an average of $8.80 an hour. That same year, the total compensation of Walmart's CEO, Michael Duke, was $18.7 million. The wealth of the Walton family, which owned the lion's share of Walmart stock, exceeded the wealth of the bottom 40 percent of American families combined.

Nor can households borrow as before. Banks and other lenders that got burned are far more careful. In addition, lending standards have tightened, and new bank regulations and overseers require prudence. Gone forever are many of the loan products of the wild years—credit cards awarded to anyone who could stand up straight, regardless of credit history; mortgages requiring no down payment; home equity loans for the asking. Housing values will not regain their speculative peak for a long time, which means homeowners cannot use their homes as sources of easy money through home equity loans and refinancing deals.

Meanwhile, a large number of Americans must get out from under the huge pile of debt they amassed. With shrunken family budgets and precarious jobs, they can't afford the interest charges. Even those who are better off are wary; the Great Recession served as a traumatic reminder that good times don't last forever. The result is that Americans are paying off, paying down, or walking away from trillions of dollars of outstanding loans—in a vast "deleveraging" of household finances that is likely to continue for years. Even as the economy returns, people won't want to be burdened by much additional debt.

At the same time, tens of millions of boomers are approaching retirement with nest eggs that have shrunk considerably, and it will take years until the values of their 401(k) plans catch up to where they had been expected to be by retirement time. In 2009, some 50 million workers lost a total of at least $1 trillion in their 401(k) plans, according to the Center for Retirement Research at Boston College. Even though the stock market has returned to its 2007 levels, boomers have lost years of gains they were counting on to boost their savings. These boomers must now save like mad. Many will have to put off retirement, which means fewer opportunities for younger people looking for work.

All this means relatively less middle-class consumption than before the Great Recession. Although consumers have to replace cars, appliances, and other things that run out or wear out or finally break down, and businesses have to replace inventories that become so depleted they have nothing left to sell or ship, a lasting and vigorous recovery cannot be based on replacements.

In mid-2009, analysts from Bank of America Merrill Lynch reported that the wealthiest 10 percent of Americans "should have enough spending power to fuel a recovery." The report's authors reasoned that before the Great Recession, the top 10 percent had accounted for more than 40 percent of consumer spending. And the recession hadn't battered this group nearly as badly as it did the middle class because the top 10 percent had most of its assets in the stock market, while the major assets of the middle class were their homes. The value of their homes had plummeted more than the Dow, and would recover more slowly.

Specious analyses like this are consistent with those produced by the much-vaunted Wall Street "talent" that plunged the nation into financial crisis. Apparently it never occurred to the authors that the only reason the top 10 percent accounted for some 40 percent of consumer spending before the Great Recession is they were taking home about 50 percent of total income, and that no "recovery" could be "fueled" by just 40 percent of prior spending.

Where will sufficient demand come from without a buoyant American middle class? Absent their spending, companies have less incentive to buy new equipment or software, or acquire new commercial buildings or factories. Without enough demand, entrepreneurs won't embark on new research or develop new products and services. It is possible, of course, that someone will introduce a new product or software application so revolutionary as to require that every business in the world buy it, thereby electrifying the economy and creating a great gush of new jobs, as did the Internet and the dot-com booms of the 1990s. But without a change in the fundamentals, a positive jolt like this is unlikely to alter the economy's long-term trajectory, as we saw when the dot-com bubble burst. Government can fill the gap for a time, but government cannot continue indefinitely to stimulate the economy with deficit spending or by printing money.

Some experts and policymakers believe the answer will be found in consumers outside the United States, especially in China. But they are wrong.

10

Why China Won't Save Us

September 24, 2009. As world leaders arrive in Pittsburgh for the Group of Twenty summit, President Obama speaks of the urgency of "rebalancing" world growth, especially between the two economic colossi of the United States and China. "We cannot go back," he says, "to an era where the Chinese . . . just are selling everything to us, we're taking out a bunch of credit card debt or home equity loans, but we're not selling anything to them." The president slightly exaggerates for effect, but his meaning is clear: Americans, he asserts, can no longer keep buying from China on credit supplied by China. The long-term fix is to get Americans to save more, and Asians—especially the Chinese—to spend more.

By this view, Chinese consumers will make up for the incapacity of American consumers to keep the U.S. economy going. By 2012, China had overtaken Japan as the world's second-largest economy, after the United States. The Chinese market is potentially huge, we are told, and its middle class is growing. Inevitably, the U.S. dollar will decline. So eventually everything we buy from them will cost us so much more and everything they buy from us so much less that we'll start exporting to them big-time. Detroit may even reemerge as the world's automobile capital. Our steel mills will be humming again. Appliance manufacturers will be resurrected on American soil. New technologies for energy efficiency and noncarbon fuels will be produced in the United States for export abroad.

This is wishful thinking.

True, the Chinese market is growing at a fast clip. By 2012, China was second only to the United States in computer sales, for example, with a larger proportion of first-time buyers. It sold more desktop computers than were sold in the United States. It had more cell-phone users. Excluding SUVs, the Chinese bought more cars than Americans did (as recently as 2006, Americans bought twice as many), more refrigerators, and more washing machines. If the Chinese economy continues to grow at or near its current rate, and the benefits of that growth trickle down to 1.3 billion Chinese consumers, the country will become the largest shopping bazaar in the history of the world. By 2050, they'll be driving over a billion cars—almost 50 percent more than the current world total—and will have become the world's biggest purchasers of household electronics, clothing, appliances, and almost everything else produced on the planet.

But the benefits of China's growth are not trickling down nearly this fast. Consumer spending there is growing far more slowly than the overall economy. The share of national income going to households in the form of wage and investment incomes continues to drop, while the share going to Chinese companies increases. In 2012, total personal consumption in China amounted to only 35 percent of the economy. Ten years earlier it was almost 50 percent. Investment, by contrast, rose from 35 percent to 44 percent of the economy. Most new jobs were in production and not, as in the United States, in retail sales or services.

Chinese companies are plowing their rising profits back into more production—additional factories, more equipment, new technologies. In 2009, the Chinese government jolted the domestic economy with a whopping package of government spending equal to $585 billion, almost as large as America's stimulus but far larger as a proportion of China's economy. But most of it was also directed at further enlarging China's capacity to produce—railways, roads, power grids, sewers, and factories. China's capital spending is on the way to exceeding that of the United States. Its consumer spending is barely a sixth as large.

China is heading in the opposite direction of "rebalancing." Its production of goods keeps soaring, but China's own consumers are taking home a shrinking proportion of the output. The destinations for what China makes are other nations, especially the United States and Europe.

Many explanations have been offered for the parsimony of Chinese consumers. Social safety nets are still inadequate, so Chinese families have to cover the costs of health care, education, and retirement. (China recently doubled its spending on these services, but the total is still low by international standards—around 6 percent of the Chinese economy, compared with an average of 25 percent in most developed nations.) Young Chinese men outnumber young Chinese women by a wide margin, so households with sons have to save and accumulate enough assets to compete successfully in the marriage market. Chinese society is aging quickly because the government has kept a tight lid on population growth for three decades. That means households are supporting lots of elderly dependents and must save in anticipation of supporting even more.

The larger explanation for Chinese frugality is that the nation is oriented toward production, not consumption. Production gives meaning and purpose to the Chinese economy. China wants to become the world's preeminent producer nation. It also wants to take the lead in the production of advanced technologies.

The United States would like to retain the lead, but our economy is oriented toward consumption rather than production. Deep down inside the cerebral cortex of our national consciousness we assume that the basic purpose of an economy is to provide more opportunities to consume. We grudgingly support government efforts to rebuild our infrastructure. We want our companies to invest in new equipment and technologies, but we also want them to pay generous dividends. We approve of government investments in basic research and development, but mainly for the purpose of making the nation more secure through advanced military technologies. (We regard spillovers to the private sector as incidental.)

China's industrial and technology policy is unapologetically direct. China especially wants America's know-how. The best way to capture know-how is to get it firsthand. So China continues to allow many U.S. and foreign companies to sell their wares there on the condition that production take place in China—often in joint ventures with Chinese companies. Even as the U.S. government was bailing out General Motors and Chrysler, the two firms' sales in China were soaring—in 2009, GM's sales there were up 67 percent from the year before, and it sold more cars in China than in the United States—but almost all the cars are made there. Procter & Gamble is so well established in China that many Chinese think its products (such as green-tea-flavored Crest toothpaste) are local brands. They might as well be. P&G makes most of them there.

By 2012, other American firms were helping China build a "smart" infrastructure, tackle pollution with clean technologies, develop a new generation of photovoltaics that convert solar radiation into electricity and wind turbines, find new applications for "nanotechnologies," and build commercial jets and jet engines. General Motors announced that it was planning to make a new subcompact in China designed and developed with its Chinese partners at the Pan-Asia Technical Automotive Center. General Electric was producing wind turbine components in China. Massachusetts-based Evergreen Solar, a leader in the production of solar panels, revealed that it was moving its plant from Devens, Massachusetts, to Wuhan, China. Applied Materials, the world's largest supplier of equipment to make solar panels, moved both its chief technology officer and its newest research lab to Xian, China.

In addition to becoming the world's center of high-tech production, China wants to create more jobs in China. That means it will continue to maintain the yuan's fixed relationship to the U.S. dollar rather than allow the yuan to rise freely against the dollar. China will allow its currency to rise a bit from time to time in order to deflect foreign criticism, but will keep it undervalued. (If the yuan rose, Chinese exports would become more expensive for us and we'd buy fewer.) This is costly for China. Not only does it keep the prices of everything China might want to import artificially high, but it also requires that when the dollar drops in international currency markets, China has to sell yuan and add to its pile of foreign assets. Yet China is willing to bear these costs because its export policy doubles as a social policy, designed to maintain order. Each year, tens of millions of poor Chinese stream into China's large cities from the countryside in pursuit of better-paying work. If they don't find it, China risks riots and other upheaval. Massive disorder is one of the greatest risks facing China's governing elite. That elite would much rather create jobs, even at the high cost of subsidizing foreign buyers, than allow the yuan to rise against the dollar and thereby risk job shortages at home.

For all these reasons, the task of "rebalancing" trade between the United States and China is far more complicated, and less likely to succeed, than is commonly admitted. The awkward truth that's not openly discussed on either side of the Pacific is that both the United States and China are capable of producing far more than their own consumers are capable of buying. In the

United States, the root of the problem, as we've seen, is a growing share of total income going to the richest Americans. Inequality is also widening in China, but the root of the problem there is a declining share of the fruits of economic growth going to average Chinese and an increasing share going to capital investment. Both societies are threatened by the disconnect between production and consumption. In China, the threat is civil unrest. In the United States, it is a prolonged jobs and earnings recession, which, when combined with widening inequality, could create a negative political backlash.

To be sure, citizens of other nations might respond to a declining dollar by buying more from the United States and thereby generating more American jobs—if the dollar were to drop far enough. But this could lead to fewer jobs in these nations, which would not be politically popular there. It is risky for any nation, especially one as large as the United States, to rely on currency adjustments as its major jobs policy; this approach can unleash competitive devaluations. Moreover, even if Americans were to gain some jobs through a weakening dollar, our export sector would have to become far larger than it has been in recent memory before American exports could make up for a big portion of the jobs already lost. And even then, the consequence would be for most Americans to become poorer as everything we purchase from the rest of the world costs that much more. It is no great feat to create jobs by growing poorer. In one way or another— through pay cuts, losses of high-paying jobs, and the substitution of lower-paying ones—we have been doing that for years.

11

No Return to Normal

It should be apparent that there will be no return to "normal," because the old normal got us into our present predicament and can't possibly get us out. So what comes next?

In order to fix what needs fixing, we need to be clear about what broke. The underlying problem is not that financial institutions were reckless, although they were. The ultimate solution, therefore, isn't just to make them more prudent. Nor is the central problem that consumers borrowed too much, although they did. The solution, therefore, isn't merely to get Americans to save more and consume less.

To summarize: The fundamental problem is that Americans no longer have the purchasing power to buy what the U.S. economy is capable of producing. The reason is that a larger and larger portion of total income has been going to the top. What's broken is the basic bargain linking pay to production. The solution is to remake the bargain.

President Obama brought the economy back from the brink. His bank rescue and stimulus packages, combined with the Fed's low interest rates, prevented the Great Recession from turning into another Great Depression. But the nation has not recommitted itself to the basic bargain. The 2010 health reform legislation was a step in the right direction but small in relation to the overall challenge. Consequently, most Americans will continue to experience relatively high unemployment and flat or declining real wages. Economic growth will be hampered.

Growth, it should be noted, is not an end in itself. It is a means to better lives for all, generating not only higher incomes and possibilities for more personal consumption but also making room for the consumption of public improvements that benefit all—an atmosphere less polluted by carbon, good schools, better health care. Rapid growth also smoothes the way toward the basic bargain: When the economy is growing nicely, the wealthy more easily accept a smaller share of its gains because they can still come out ahead of where they were before. Simultaneously, when everyone else enjoys a larger share, they more willingly pay taxes to support public improvements. It's a virtuous cycle.

Slow or no growth has the reverse effect. Economic gains are so meager that the wealthy fight harder to maintain their share. The middle class, already burdened by high unemployment and flat or dropping wages, fights ever more furiously against any additional burdens, such as tax increases to support public schools or price increases resulting from regulations limiting carbon emissions. It's a vicious cycle.

The question, then, is how to move from a vicious cycle to a virtuous one—how to restore the widespread prosperity needed for growth, and how to get the growth necessary for widespread prosperity. The challenge is both economic and political. A fundamentally new economy is required—the next stage of capitalism. But how will we get there? And what will it look like when we do?

There are essentially two paths from here. Only one will get us to where we want to be.

PART II

Backlash

1

The 2020 Election

November 3, 2020. The newly formed Independence Party pulls enough votes away from both the Republican and Democratic candidates to give its own candidate, Margaret Jones, a plurality of votes, an electoral college victory, and the presidency. A significant number of Independence Party members have also taken seats away from Democrats and Republicans in Congress.

The platform of the Independence Party, as well as its message, is clear and uncompromising: zero tolerance of illegal immigrants; a freeze on legal immigration from Latin America, Africa, and Asia; increased tariffs on all imports; a ban on American companies moving their operations to another country or outsourcing abroad; a prohibition on foreign "sovereign wealth funds" investing in the United States. America will withdraw from the United Nations, the World Trade Organization, the World Bank, and the International Monetary Fund; end all "involvements" in foreign countries; refuse to pay any more interest on our debt to China, essentially defaulting on it; and stop trading with China unless China freely floats its currency.

Profitable companies will be prohibited from laying off workers and cutting payrolls. The federal budget must always be balanced. The Federal Reserve will be abolished.

Banks will be allowed only to take deposits and make loans. Investment banking will be prohibited. Anyone found to have engaged in insider trading, stock manipulation, or securities fraud will face imprisonment for no less than ten years.

Finally, but not least: In order for the government to balance the budget, provide for national defense, guard our borders, and pay down the national debt, all personal incomes will be capped at $500,000 per year; earnings in excess of that amount will be taxed at 100 percent. Incomes above $250,000 are to be taxed at 80 percent. The capital gains rate will be 80 percent. All net worth above $100,000 will be subject to a 2 percent annual wealth tax. Any American found to be sheltering his income in a foreign nation will be stripped of his U.S. citizenship.

In her victory speech, president-elect Jones is defiant:

My fellow Americans: You have voted to reclaim America. Voted to take it back from big government, big business, and big finance. To take it back from the politicians who would rob us of our freedoms, from foreigners who rob us of our jobs, from the rich who have no loyalty to this nation, and from immigrants who live off our hard work. (*Wild applause.*) We are reclaiming America from the elites who have rigged the system to their benefit, from the money manipulators on Wall Street and the greed masters in corporate executive suites, from the influence peddlers and pork peddlers in Washington—from all the privileged and the powerful who have conspired against us. (*Wild applause and cheers.*) They will no longer sell Americans out to global money and pad their nests by taking away our jobs and livelihoods! (*Wild applause, cheers.*) This is our nation, now! (*Wild applause and cheers that continue to build.*) A nation of good jobs and good wages for anyone willing to work hard! Our nation! America for Americans! (*Thunderous applause.*)

Her opponents' concession speeches are bitter. George P. Bush, the Republican candidate, is irate. "I cannot stand before you and congratulate my opponent, who based her entire campaign on fear and resentment," he tells his supporters.

Chelsea Clinton, the Democratic candidate, is indignant. "I would very much like to offer Margaret Jones my best wishes for the future. But I have to be honest: She and the Independence Party pose a grave danger to this nation."

Foreign leaders try to be respectful but cannot hide their anxieties. The British prime minister issues a terse statement "wishing Americans well." The German chancellor offers "condolences," but the German ambassador to the United States insists the chancellor's remark has been mistranslated and is best understood as "commiserations." The president of China appears before news cameras and says, simply, "The United States has committed a grave error."

The presidents of the U.S. Chamber of Commerce and the Business Roundtable issue a joint statement warning that Margaret Jones and the Independence Party "will push America into another Great Depression." The CEOs of the four remaining giant Wall Street firms predict economic collapse.

On November 4, the day after Election Day, the Dow Jones Industrial Average drops 50 percent in an unprecedented volume of trading. The dollar plummets 30 percent against a weighted average of other currencies. Wall Street is in a panic. Banks close. Business leaders predict economic calamity. Mainstream pollsters, pundits, and political consultants fill the airwaves with expressions of shock and horror. Over and over again, they ask: How could this have happened?

2

The Politics of Economics, 2010–2020

How indeed. To get some insight, let's examine what could very well occur in the decade preceding the election of Margaret Jones.

History teaches us that politics is inextricably bound up with economics. Presidents are not nearly as responsible for the economy as voters assume, but they are held accountable nonetheless. Jimmy Carter lost his bid for reelection in 1980 because the economy had been suffering double-digit inflation, mostly brought on by soaring oil prices. In order to "break the back of inflation," as it was put, Paul Volcker, then chairman of the Fed—but obviously also no Marriner Eccles—raised interest rates so high that he also broke the back of the economy, pushing unemployment into the stratosphere. That also broke the back of the administration. Voters blamed Carter and elected Ronald Reagan.

Reagan, by contrast, won reelection handily in 1984, largely because the economy was surging by then, and voters credited him. George Bush lost his reelection bid in 1992, this time at the hands of Alan Greenspan. Greenspan raised interest rates to ward off inflation, which also raised unemployment. Voters blamed Bush and in 1992 gave Bill Clinton a plurality of votes because he promised to fix the economy. (In the words of his colorful political advisor, James Carville, "It's the economy, stupid.") Clinton was reelected in 1996 mainly because jobs were returning. Barack Obama won in 2008 as the economy teetered precariously on the edge of a precipice. Many blamed the bad economy on George W. Bush, and that blame spilled over to John McCain, the Republican candidate. (In 2004, Bush won reelection mainly because of the "War on Terror.") In the 2010 midterm elections, with the economy still reeling from the Great Recession, blame shifted to President Obama and the Democrats. Republicans retook control of the House of Representatives and gained seats in the Senate. In 2012, with the economy slightly improved, Democrats regained some ground and Obama was reelected. All that can be said with confidence is that jobs and the economy are almost always at the forefront of voters' minds.

But even accepting the powerful effect of the economy, a backlash on the scale of my hypothetical scenario would have as much to do with voters' cumulative frustrations and pent-up anger as with specific economic conditions on Election Day. It is not difficult to foresee a plausible trajectory. For the reasons enumerated in Part I, after the stimulus ends and the Federal Reserve tightens the money supply and raises interest rates, and after businesses replenish inventories and consumers replace worn-out products, the jobs machine stalls, and economic growth slows. Over the slightly longer term, more companies decide that their American employees are overpaid relative to equally productive workers elsewhere in the world working at a fraction of American wages, or to readily available software and automated equipment. Consequently, large numbers of middle-class Americans have to accept lower pay if they want to stay employed. With their coping mechanisms in shatters, they have to face a necessity they have managed to avoid for decades: They have to make do with less.

Poor families with minimum education are especially hardhit. The middle class adapts in various ways. More young middle-class adults choose to live with their parents and delay marriage and children. Most Americans search harder for bargains, buy more private-label groceries and generic drugs, settle for lower grades of meat at the supermarket, stay home more, and take fewer vacations. Many give up second cars, and consequently depend more on public transportation. A significant number grow their own food, do their own home repairs, and mend their own clothes.

This permanent frugality will not come naturally. According to common stereotypes, the French draw deep satisfaction from good food and wine, the Germans from music, the English from their parks, and Americans from shopping. These facile generalizations are not entirely baseless. Just before the Great Recession, personal consumption in America equaled almost 70 percent of the country's gross domestic product (more than 75 percent if you include the purchases of homes). By contrast, personal consumption constituted only 65 percent of the British economy, 55 percent of Germany's, and 52 percent of Japan's. (Personal consumption did not always constitute 70 percent of the American economy. During the Great Prosperity of 1947–1975, it held fairly steady at 62 percent, without noticeable concern. But the economy was different then. As I said earlier, income and wealth were far more equitably shared. And most Americans were on an upward trajectory.)

Yet frugality itself is unlikely to ignite a political firestorm. We have had to pull in our belts before. To understand why Margaret Jones and the Independence Party (or their reasonable facsimile) could take control, we need a deeper understanding of the confluence between economics, politics, and behavior.

3

Why Can't We Be Content with Less?

Historically, America's cultural obsession to consume has been tempered by the "higher virtues" of thrift and self-sufficiency. "Be industrious and frugal, and you will be rich," advised Benjamin Franklin. The simple life has been viewed as honorable. "Many of the so-called comforts of life, are not only not indispensable," wrote Henry David Thoreau in 1854, "but positive hindrances to the elevation of mankind." Even after the introduction of mass production and mass marketing, as Americans swooned over the tantalizing vision of the nation as cornucopia of consumer delight, many eschewed crass materialism. "The people of this country need a . . . philosophy of living, not having; of happiness, not wealth," noted John Ellsworth, Jr., in *The North American Review* of October 1932, in the depths of the Great Depression.

Years ago, University of Illinois psychologist Ed Diener surveyed winners of state lotteries and some of the richest Americans (identified by *Forbes* as among the wealthiest one hundred). They expressed only slightly greater happiness than did the average American, and much of their happiness proved to be temporary. People in other countries and cultures are much the same. University of Michigan researcher Ronald Inglehart examined 256,000 people in seventeen different nations and found barely any connection between income and happiness, above a subsistence level. It turns out that what money buys has rapidly diminishing emotional returns. Once we've enjoyed something, the next experience of it is not quite as wonderful, and the third might even be humdrum. As long as we're not destitute, happiness is less about getting what we want than about appreciating what we already have.

Much of what people want can't be bought anyway. In 1943, behavioral scientist Abraham Maslow wrote "A Theory of Human Motivation," a paper in which he posited a hierarchy of human needs. At the bottom are food, shelter, sex, and sleep (of which the first two are typically purchased, although markets also exist for the latter two). Next come safety and security (which we normally purchase as well, typically through locks on the doors and taxes that pay for police officers and a system of criminal justice). If we lack any of these basics, we're forced to spend most of our time trying to remedy what's missing. But once these fundamental needs are met, according to Maslow, our higher needs cannot be satisfied in the market—indeed, the very act of trying to purchase them robs them of their emotional sustenance. They include "belonging needs," such as love, acceptance, and affiliation, and "esteem needs," by which he meant self-respect, social status, and the approval of others. At the top of Maslow's pyramid are "self-actualization" needs—our yearning to find meaning in our lives and to express ourselves.

By some measures, then, one could argue that with less paid work and less money to spend, people could—at least theoretically—enjoy their simpler lives. Before the Great Recession, many Americans were trying to cope with declining hourly wages by working more hours and sleeping less—by some estimates an average of one or two fewer hours each night than in the 1960s. (That deprivation created an entirely new industry. In 2007, Americans spent a whopping $23.9 billion on sleep-related products and services—everything from white-noise machines and special sleep-inducing mattresses to drugs for insomnia. That was more than double what we spent on sleep a decade before, according to Marketdata Enterprises, a research firm in Tampa, Florida.)

In mid-2009, the *Archives of General Psychiatry* released a study showing that one in ten Americans take antidepressants within the course of a year, making antidepressants the most prescribed medication in the nation, and by extension, in history. The number of Americans on antidepressants doubled between 1997 and 2007, even as the stock market and home values soared. Antidepressants surely help millions of people cope with stressful lives, but some of the stresses of that era came from trying to earn enough to afford everything that was considered the hallmark of a successful life.

The harder we worked to buy these things, the less time and energy we had to enjoy what we bought. American culture sent an increasingly mixed message: Work like mad but enjoy life to the fullest. Doing both proved impossible. Sociologist Daniel Bell identified this cultural contradiction years ago, but it became more pronounced in the years preceding the Great Recession. The Protestant virtues of hard work and deferred gratification were at increasing odds with a market that instructed us to fulfill our dreams instantly and indulge our every want. As those wants continuously ratcheted upward—fueled by our anxieties over aging, relative status, and personal attractiveness—we worked even harder.

The argument on behalf of hard work has always been premised on something of a lie. People are led to believe that one day they will find satisfaction, if not in the work itself, when they finally have worked hard enough to afford and accumulate what they desire. But that day never seems to arrive. There is no light at the end of the acquisitive tunnel. Even Adam Smith, the putative father of market economics, recognized the centrality of this deception. Writing in the eighteenth century (not in his *Wealth of Nations* but in his *Theory of Moral Sentiments*), he described the typical worker who "through the whole of his life ... pursues the idea of a certain artificial and elegant repose which he may never arrive at, for which he sacrifices a real tranquillity. . . . It is this deception which rouses and keeps in continual motion the industry of mankind."

A simpler life may prove to be safer as well. Almost 10 percent fewer people were killed on America's highways in the bust year of 2009 than in the boom year of 2007, according to the National Highway Traffic Safety Administration. Some credit safer cars, but that can't be right, because cars weren't that much safer in 2009 than they were in 2007. In fact, they were mostly the same cars, because sales of new cars plummeted. Some hypothesize that our roads became safer, but there is no evidence of this, either. (Actually, many of them are falling apart for lack of adequate maintenance, and major bridges are still caving in.) Some think the drop in highway fatalities was due to drivers' being more careful—buckling their seat belts, obeying traffic laws. That would be nice if it were true, but here too the evidence is weak. Seat-belt laws had been in effect in most states for years. If anything, we were less careful, chatting on cell phones, texting, fiddling with BlackBerrys and iPhones, and adjusting global positioning devices. And more of us have been driving motorcycles and scooters, accounting for a growing number of highway deaths.

The salient reason for these statistics is much simpler. When the economy slows, fewer people take to the roads. Fewer commute to work, fewer pick up and deliver, fewer drive from one client or meeting to another. And as incomes shrink, fewer people drive to malls, movies, and restaurants because they have less money to spend. Fewer people on the highways means fewer highway accidents and deaths.

The same phenomenon can be traced to the workplace, where deaths and serious injuries dropped to their lowest rates on record in 2009, according to the Department of Labor. This wasn't because workplaces suddenly became safer, workers more careful, or inspectors more diligent. It was because employers trimmed back hours, particularly in risky professions like construction, where the fatality rate dropped 20 percent. The bursting housing bubble meant far fewer workers on roofs, under cranes, and behind electric saws, where they might be severely injured or killed.

Greenhouse gas emissions also dropped in 2009. That wasn't because environmental regulations mandated it. Nor was it because people suddenly became more environmentally conscious. Emissions dropped because consumption declined in the United States and in many other places around the world, thereby reducing production and usage of everything that emitted carbon dioxide. In all likelihood, this improved the health of Americans, as well as that of others around the planet.

Given all these palpable benefits, it is not implausible that Americans will find more contentment as we consume less. But this sanguine prognosis ignores several painful adjustments we will have to make.

4

The Pain of Economic Loss

The first painful adjustment will be to a lower standard of living—or at least far lower than we anticipated. Behavioral research shows that losses are more painful than gains are pleasurable. Most people won't take a bet that gives them an 85 percent chance of doubling their life savings and a 15 percent chance of losing them. In a similar vein, most of us put a higher premium on the cost of giving up something than we do on receiving an item in the first place. Princeton psychologist Daniel Kahneman demonstrated this by placing people into two randomly selected groups. Those in the first group were shown a particular type of mug and asked how much they'd be willing to pay for it. Those in the second were given the mug and then asked how much money they'd want in order to give it back. It turned out that people in the second group demanded twice as much to part with the mug as those in the first group were willing to pay for it.

Gains and losses aren't symmetrical, because whatever we possess sets a minimum standard for how we judge our material well-being thereafter. When we lose something of value, we retain the memory of having once had it, and regret the loss. If we lose a convenience or a benefit that we relied on, even worse: We must also forego our dependence on it. Someone who's enjoyed the benefit of an air conditioner and then has to do without because he can't afford to fix it after it breaks, for example, is likely to feel much worse off than someone who could never afford air-conditioning in the first place.

Societies whose living standards drop experience higher levels of stress than do societies that never had as much to begin with— and the deeper the drop, the higher the stress. Suicide rates offer some evidence. When even a wealthy economy like the United States dips, the rate of suicides rises; the longer the downturn lasts, the higher the rate becomes. Behavioral economist Christopher Ruhm found that for every 1 percent rise in a state's unemployment rate, the number of suicides increases 1.3 percent. If people remain jobless for long, the suicide rate rises further. The stock market crash of 1929 caused an increase in suicides, and the suicide rate rose as the Great Depression wore on. In 1929, there were 15.3 suicides for every hundred thousand people; by 1930, 17 per hundred thousand; by 1932, 18.6.

An extreme example of the social and psychological stresses accompanying prolonged economic loss occurred in Germany after World War I, when most Germans became far poorer than they were before. The Treaty of Versailles required Germany to pay the Allies substantial sums in reparations for the cost of the war, making it difficult for Germany to rebuild and subjecting it to continued economic distress, including hyperinflation in the 1920s followed by widespread unemployment. By the time Adolf Hitler made his political debut, many Germans were eager to turn to anyone who seemed to offer a solution to the problems they had long endured, as well as an easy scapegoat.

Perhaps the hardest loss for middle-class Americans will be giving up the expectation that the future has to be materially better. We're used to moving up in America, surpassing ourselves, trading up. Middle-class Americans have long assumed that hard work will ensure a better future for them and, especially, for their children. But by 2013, polls showed that a majority of Americans thought their children would be worse off.

The last time our hopes for a better life were dashed so profoundly was during the Great Depression. Robert and Helen Lynd, the sociologists I mentioned earlier who studied Muncie, Indiana, in 1924 and then wrote *Middletown,* returned in 1934 to see if anything had changed. Their report, published as *Middletown in Transition,* noted that the "staggering, traumatic effect" of "the great knife of the depression" was to end the hopes of Muncie's citizens to own their own homes, send their kids to college, and do better than their parents did. The Depression also made them continuously fearful of sliding farther backward. The disappointment and anxiety resembled, in the Lynds' words, "the crisis quality of a serious illness, when life's customary busy immediacies drop away and one lies helplessly confronting oneself, reviewing the past, and asking abrupt questions of the future." As one housewife remarked, "The march backwards entails many things that leave a bitter taste."

My grandfather Alexander Reich was a wealthy man before the Great Depression but lost everything in the Crash of 1929. He moved his family out of a brownstone in New York City and into a small apartment. Although he initially believed he'd be able to regain lost ground, as the Depression wore on he gradually lost his faith. He tried other businesses but never succeeded. My memory of him from the 1950s is of a man filled with sadness and regret. For him, the American dream had been shattered.

Yet even so, my grandfather's despair did not make him angry with the economic system or with the political or business leadership of the country. He was mostly angry with himself. So were countless others who had been caught in the sharp downdraft of the Great Depression. Will it be any different in the coming years? The economic conditions most Americans will experience may cause them disappointment and anxiety, to be sure, but will that turn them into angry reactionaries? That certainly doesn't have to be the case.

5

Adding Insult to Injury

The second painful adjustment for most people will be to a standard of living that's even more significantly lower than that attained by America's rich. Social psychologists have long understood that people typically measure their own well-being by comparison to how others are doing. When the incomes of people at the top soar and they live better as a result, everyone else feels a bit poorer. This psychological truth is likely to become more important. While Americans have suffered economic reversals before, and the middle class has felt deprived relative to those at the top, the years ahead are likely to mark the first time Americans will experience both together.

America's rich did take a hit in the Crash of 2008. According to *Forbes* magazine, the nation's four hundred wealthiest people lost about $300 billion that year. That still left those four hundred enough to live on, though—a total of $1.27 trillion (more than the estimated cost of achieving universal health care for the entire nation for the next decade). The median pay of CEOs at America's five hundred largest companies dropped 15 percent that year, to $7.3 million. Pay and benefits at Wall Street's biggest banks dropped nearly 11 percent. It was not all bad news, however. New York's attorney general found that nearly five thousand of Wall Street's "top performers" still received multimillion-dollar bonuses that year. And a study by *The Wall Street Journal* found that the retirement plans of a quarter of the top executives at major companies actually increased in value, even as most of their employees' 401(k)s declined precipitously. The executives' employment contracts guaranteed them fixed returns.

Yet by the end of 2012, most of the rich had bounced back, and the gap between them and everyone else was widening again. One major reason: Most of the assets of rich Americans are held in stocks, bonds, and other financial instruments—whose values rose in the wake of the Great Recession as companies cut costs (especially their U.S. payrolls) and expanded their global operations. By contrast, as noted earlier, the major asset of middle-class Americans has been their homes, whose prices took a beating in the downturn and, in most parts of the country, won't return to their 2007 levels for many years. Beyond this was the inexorable trend of corporations' cutting the jobs and pay of anyone who could be replaced by foreign workers or by software and automated machinery, while competing for the "talent" who pushed profits higher.

In early 2010, only a little more than a year after the crash, Wall Street awarded pay packages as if the crash had never occurred. JPMorgan Chase more than doubled its profits from 2008, generating record revenues and paying out $27 billion to its already well-heeled executives, traders, and other "vital" employees. Goldman Sachs posted its largest profit in history and distributed $16.2 billion in bonuses. (Goldman could have paid out bigger bonuses but, concerned about its tarnished public image, held back. According to *The New York Times,* Goldman's employees accepted the less-than-anticipated payout but soon expected to be rewarded for going along with what one characterized as "a temporary public relations exercise.") Even though some of the worst abuses of the boom years had been contained, the Street effectively resisted congressional efforts to tie its collective hands. It was still making large global bets with other people's money and taking in giant fees regardless of how those bets turned out. Few financial trends are as certain as the outsized rewards the denizens of Wall Street will continue to claim as their rightful winnings.

The compensation packages awarded to corporate CEOs and executives likewise continued to soar. Here again, top executive pay was on the same trajectory it had been on before the Great Recession, as if almost nothing had happened in the intervening time. Executive pay was linked to the profitability and stock market performance of their companies. Both were on the rise, reflecting the increasing ease with which payrolls could be cut and the work automated or parceled out overseas, and also the telling fact that many foreign markets were emerging from recession more rapidly than the United States. The race for executive "talent" had also become more global. Big companies continued to raise executive pay in order to attract the best from around the world, who in turn continued to scour the globe for great deals and new markets. This trend will surely endure. Astonishingly, the twenty-five leading hedge-fund managers did far better than even investment bankers and top corporate executives, raking in an average of $1 billion each, as I've noted.

Yet the majority of Americans will continue to battle obsolescence—competing ever more furiously with workers around the world as well as with new generations of software. Unless action is taken to reverse these trends, the share of national income going to the top will continue to grow and the share going to everyone else will continue to decline.

Many of the things people want are valuable in relation to what other people have. Indeed, much of the idea of "value" is related to the social role we're playing. As economist Richard Layard has written, "In a poor society a man proves to his wife that he loves her by giving her a rose, but in a rich society he must give her a dozen roses." You can see this most graphically in computer-based simulated worlds, where many people seem to get almost as much satisfaction from paying real money for "virtual" goods—tiny icons representing designer clothes or fancy cars—as they do from buying the genuine articles in the real world, at a much higher cost. In these simulated worlds, the virtual goods serve a similar social function as the real ones, establishing one's relative wealth—and worth.

Relativity accounts for what's seen as a "luxury" and what's a "necessity." As far back as the eighteenth century, Adam Smith defined necessities as "not only the commodities which are indispensably necessary for the support of life, but whatever the custom of the country renders it indecent for creditable people, even of the lowest order, to be without." In most of eighteenth-century Europe, a linen shirt was not strictly speaking a necessity, but Smith noted that a common laborer would be ashamed to appear in public without one, "the want of which would be supposed to denote that disgraceful degree of poverty, which, it is presumed, nobody can well fall into without extreme bad conduct." Leather shoes were a "necessity" in England for both men and women, he wrote, but only for men in Scotland, and for neither in France.

In 1899, the economist-sociologist Thorstein Veblen noted that people take their cues from those above them and seek to match their living standards with the "conspicuous consumption" of the very rich. More than a half century later, economist James Duesenberry recognized that the demand for many products has more to do with the social standing they give their purchasers than with any intrinsic value. He called it the "demonstration effect," which signals to others that the possessor of an item is wealthy enough to afford it, and thereby establishes his or her position in a social pecking order.

"Wealth," said H. L. Mencken, the American satirist of the early twentieth century, "is any income at least $100 more a year than the income of one's wife's sister's husband." Times have changed and many women are now breadwinners, but a family's relative position (and not just compared to one's relatives) still matters. Yet the desire to do better when the incomes of people at the top are rising is not just due to envy or any other character flaw on most people's parts. It's connected to an implicit upward shift in the social norm of what constitutes a good life. Even people whose incomes haven't actually dropped feel deprived relative to how those at the top now live; people whose incomes have dropped feel even poorer.

The evidence is all around us. People who live in states where incomes are more equal register higher levels of satisfaction than do people where the gap is wider. The same holds among nations. Scandinavians express more contentment with their lot in life than do inhabitants of southern Europe, where inequality is higher. Researchers have found that inequality correlates with health, for much the same reason. Richard Wilkinson of the University of Nottingham, in England, has discovered that once economic growth lifts a country out of extreme poverty, its citizens are likely to live longer and healthier lives—as long as there are not large differences in their incomes. The inhabitants of poorer countries with more equal incomes are sometimes healthier, on average, than are the citizens of richer countries whose incomes are more unequal.

Even people whose incomes rise feel less satisfied than beforehand when they are exposed to others whose incomes are much higher. After the Berlin Wall tumbled, living standards for the former inhabitants of East Germany soared, but their level of contentment declined. The reason: They began comparing themselves to West Germans rather than to others in the Soviet bloc.

Few middle-class people aspire to live in a forty-four-thousand-square-foot mansion like the one Bill Gates built for himself near Seattle. But by building that mansion, Gates set a new norm for other exceedingly wealthy people, some of whom subsequently built mansions just as big. These giant mansions also ratcheted up the aspirations of people below them, who were rich rather than exceedingly wealthy, and who began building larger homes than they had ever lived in before. And so on down the income ladder, until the new norm reached the middle class.

As economist Robert H. Frank has pointed out, something like this chain of comparisons helps explain why the typical new home built in the United States in 2007 (2,500 square feet) was about 50 percent bigger than its counterpart built in 1977 (1,780 square feet), even though median incomes barely rose. A similar comparative process operated on other purchases. As the exceedingly rich threw million-dollar birthday parties and even more extravagant weddings, a chain of comparison also pushed up the price of middle-class celebrations. The typical American wedding cost $11,213 in 1980; by 2007 it cost $28,082 (both figures adjusted for inflation).

Middle-class paychecks couldn't keep up with the costs of these homes, weddings, and many other amenities, which is why so many people went so deeply into debt. But by 2008 that debt option disappeared—which may help explain why, for example, the typical new home in 2009 slipped back, to 2,392 square feet. Yet the chain of comparison has not disappeared. To the contrary, the middle class has become more acutely aware of how far it has fallen relative to the top.

The very rich may have become somewhat more guarded about displaying their opulence. During the Great Recession, conspicuous consumption became unseemly. "Shopping is a little vulgar right now," said an editor at *Allure* magazine. Yet in a world of instant and pervasive communication, the rich cannot easily hide their wealth. Shortly after Lehman Brothers went bust, *The Daily Beast* reported that Kathleen Fuld, wife of former Lehman Brothers CEO Richard Fuld, selected a plain white bag to conceal her purchase of three $2,225 cashmere scarves at an Hermès boutique in New York. One Web site, created in 2009, allows the curious to type in the name of any CEO or financial tycoon and zoom in on a bird's-eye view of their personal estates.

As income and wealth have continued to accumulate at the top, the rich have been able to buy more highly desirable things whose supply is necessarily limited. Prestigious universities have only a limited number of places, which is one way they maintain their prestige. Because those schools are often gateways to the best jobs, competition for admission is intense. As the rich have grown richer while the middle class has lost ground, children from wealthy families have been at an increasing advantage in this race: They attend high-quality private high schools (or top-ranked public high schools accessible only to families wealthy enough to live in the area they serve, which amounts to the same thing), while the quality of public schools available to most families has declined. Children of the affluent have access to private tutors to help them with difficult subjects, to test preparation services that guide them through SATs and other entrance exams, and to coaches to help assemble their applications—incurring expenses that struggling middle-class families cannot afford. Some children of the wealthy also gain favorable treatment by admissions officials because their parents are major donors to the college (or likely to become so if their child is admitted).

Increasingly, too, the most accomplished doctors and medical specialists, and the best hospitals and health care facilities, have become available only to the very rich. New health reform legislation will extend care to more people and necessarily limit what doctors and hospitals can charge, as does Medicare. For this reason, the law is unlikely to dramatically increase the supply of either. One likely result will be to increase the market price of the most desirable physicians and facilities, making them accessible mainly to those who can afford them.

Whether it's an education at a prestigious school, excellent medical care, or even gorgeous oceanfront property, anything that's desirable but in limited supply has become less accessible to the vast middle class as purchasing power has become concentrated at the top. And as the rich have simultaneously withdrawn from institutions dedicated to the common good, like public schools, they both bid up the price of desirable private ones and reduce the quality of what remains public. Increasingly, upscale towns, gated communities, and office parks are financed by fees paid by their wealthy inhabitants. Having seceded from townships or jurisdictions inhabited by the middle class and the poor, the very wealthy pay fewer local taxes to support services for those of more modest means.

As the income gap continues to widen, deprivations like these are likely to cause many Americans to feel even poorer and, in many cases, more frustrated. In other nations, at other times, wide disparities in income and wealth have led to political instability. Summarizing the research, economists Roberto Perotti and Alberto Alesina have found that "income inequality increases social discontent and fuels social unrest. The latter, by increasing the probability of coups, revolutions, [and] mass violence."

This has not been the case in America, at least not so far. Here, opulence has provoked more ambition than hostility. In this respect we are different from older cultures with feudal origins and long histories of class conflict. For most Americans, the rich have not been "them"; instead, they're people whom we aspire to become. We worry only when private wealth exercises political power. It was here that Theodore Roosevelt and Woodrow Wilson drew the line on the trusts, and Franklin D. Roosevelt damned the "economic royalists." Private wealth applied to ostentatious consumption is perfectly appropriate; applied to the purchase of political power, it becomes diabolic.

Given the chance, most members of the middle class want to join the ranks of the rich and gain all the perks that come with great wealth. The real frustration, and the final straw, will come if and when they no longer feel they have a chance because the dice are loaded against them.

6

Outrage at a Rigged Game

Americans might be able to accept a high rate of unemployment coupled with lower wages. We are likely to accommodate absolute as well as relative losses in our standard of living for a long stretch of time. We might abide even wider inequality. But when all of these are added to a perception that the economic game is rigged—that no matter how hard we try we cannot get ahead because those with great wealth and power will block our way— the combination may very well be toxic.

Losers of rigged games can become very angry. I remember when in 2009 my employer, the University of California, announced that due to state budget cuts, the salaries of all faculty and staff would have to be reduced. Most of my colleagues grudgingly accepted the outcome; we were all in roughly the same boat, and the state's budget was in crisis. But when the *San Francisco Chronicle* reported that a few top administrators at the university had gotten pay raises, all hell broke loose. Suddenly the sacrifices seemed larger and less tolerable. (In fact, the *Chronicle* exaggerated, but the damage was done.)

Something like this has been happening on a national scale. Even before the Great Recession, evidence began accumulating that the game was tilted in the direction of big business and the wealthy. Recall the busting of unions, the slashing of payrolls, and the shredding of employee benefits, without any attempt by government to constrain or reverse these practices; the junk-bond and private-equity deals that flipped companies like cards, burdened them with debt, and forced mass layoffs; the resplendent pay packages of top corporate and financial executives and traders, even as marginal taxes on the rich were cut and Wall Street was deregulated. In the 1980s, irresponsible gambles by some savings-and-loan banks cost taxpayers $125 billion; one such bank was owned by Charles Keating, who "donated" $300,000 to five U.S. senators, thereby greasing the skids with federal regulators. Insider trading scandals involving junk-bond kings including Ivan Boesky and Michael Milken did their damage. The BCCI money-laundering scandal ruined the reputation of Clark Clifford, advisor to four presidents. Then came the corporate looting scandals: In 2002, CEOs of giant corporations like Enron and WorldCom were found to have padded their nests at the expense of small investors. Other corporations that cooked their books included Adelphia, Global Crossing, Tyco, Sunbeam, and ImClone. Every major U.S. accounting firm either admitted negligence or paid substantial fines without admitting guilt. Nearly every major investment bank played a part in defrauding investors, largely by urging them to buy stocks that the bank's own analysts privately described as junk.

In the years leading up to the Crash of 2008, Wall Street made large and risky bets with other people's money. Goldman Sachs, among others, created bundles of mortgage debt and persuaded investors to buy them, hawking them as good investments. Goldman even lobbied credit-rating agencies to give the mortgage bundles high ratings as solid bets. Yet Goldman simultaneously, and quietly, bet against them—"shorting" them, in the parlance of Wall Street. When the bottom fell out of the mortgage market, Goldman made a huge profit.

Through it all, government regulators slept.

Despite all this evidence that the deck was stacked, the voting behavior of most Americans did not noticeably change. As I've noted, voting tracked the business cycle. On the upswing, we rewarded incumbents; on the downswing, we punished them. Apart from temporary bouts of unemployment at the bottom of the cycle, most Americans did not seem particularly worried by the long-term tilt of the playing field in favor of big business and Wall Street, and their ever cozier relationships with Washington. The three coping mechanisms allowed most people to achieve an adequately comfortable standard of living notwithstanding. But in the wake of the Great Recession, with their coping mechanisms gone, Americans began paying more heed. We are more sensitive to how the game is played and more upset by evidence of collusion at the top.

We are already showing signs.

The giant bailout of Wall Street was sold to the American people as a way to save Main Street and jobs. But it appeared to do neither. The bankers on Wall Street mostly saved themselves, using the taxpayers' money to keep their banks sufficiently solvent to do a new round of deals that generated them billions of dollars. Yet little or nothing trickled down to Main Street. Small businesses could not get loans. Few homeowners were able to renegotiate their mortgages, and large numbers lost their homes. Wall Street lobbied successfully against a proposal to allow homeowners to declare bankruptcy rather than forfeit their homes. The proposal would have given distressed homeowners more bargaining leverage with the banks that owned their mortgages. Not surprisingly, in a poll taken by Hart Associates in September 2009, more than 60 percent of respondents felt that "large banks" had been helped "a lot" or "a fair amount" by government economic policies, but only 13 percent felt that the "average working person" had been.

The whole thing began to look like a giant insider deal created by Wall Streeters for Wall Streeters, at everyone else's expense.

Before coming to the Treasury, Paulson had headed Goldman Sachs, one of the most successful of the big banks. Geithner had been installed in the New York Fed by major bankers, including Robert Rubin, Treasury secretary under Bill Clinton, who also had headed Goldman Sachs and was now a top executive at Citigroup. While engineering the bailout, Paulson and Geithner consulted with Lloyd Blankfein, who was then CEO of Goldman Sachs. Not coincidentally, perhaps, Citigroup and Goldman were among the largest beneficiaries of the bailout.

When Paulson and Geithner considered whether to bail out giant insurer AIG, which owed Goldman $13 billion, they consulted with Blankfein. They did not demand that Goldman (or any of the other parties to whom AIG owed money) accept a penny less than what was owed them—even though, as the inspector general who oversaw the bailout subsequently noted in a critical report, Goldman would have collected far less had AIG been forced into bankruptcy. In effect, $13 billion went from taxpayers to AIG and then promptly from AIG to Goldman— although for many months Geithner and the Treasury refused to disclose that, and Goldman refused to acknowledge it. E-mails from officials at the New York Fed instructed executives at AIG not even to disclose the payments in its public filings with the Securities and Exchange Commission. The inspector general concluded that the AIG deal "offered little opportunity for success," and left taxpayers holding the bag.

Paulson's and Geithner's subsequent actions made several of the big banks even bigger—providing Bank of America, Wells Fargo, and JPMorgan Chase additional subsidies in order to consolidate with other, weaker institutions. Furthermore, each bank was allowed to value its bad loans (most of which were unlikely to be repaid in full) at whatever price it wanted as long as it passed a so-called stress test conducted by Treasury officials, whose only information came from the banks themselves. And the Federal Reserve kept the price of money so low that the big banks could borrow it essentially free.

Not surprisingly, within a year, most of the remaining banks were hugely profitable again.

The public felt duped. And the damage done to the economy as a result of the banks' recklessness was incalculable. When Lloyd Blankfein tried to defend Goldman's giant $16 billion bonus pool for 2009 by saying the firm had been "doing God's work," he was roundly criticized. A week later he issued a formal apology, admitting that Goldman "participated in things that were clearly wrong." He did not offer to return the $13 billion that had gone from taxpayers to Goldman via AIG, however.

After the bailout, there was much talk in Washington about regulating the Street to prevent a similar collapse and bailout in the future. But the Street's army of Washington lobbyists kept new regulations to a minimum. The White House sought to charge banks for the cost of the bailout, but this hardly constituted reform; at best, it compensated for the costs of cleaning up the mess. Proposed rules to constrain the trading of derivatives— bets made on changes in the values of real assets—were riddled with loopholes big enough for bankers to drive their Ferraris through. Yet Congress did not allow distressed homeowners to declare bankruptcy.

In 2012, JP Morgan Chase, the nation's largest bank, whose chief executive, Jamie Dimon, led Wall Street's war against bank regulation, lost $6 billion due to excessively risky bets. A congressional report in 2013 found that the bank had misled the public and its investors about the losses. Nothing, it seemed, had changed.

Nor was there any enthusiasm in Congress or in the White House for using the antitrust laws to break up the biggest banks—

a traditional tonic for any capitalist entity "too big to fail." By 2012, the biggest Wall Street banks were far bigger than they had been four years before, when they were bailed out. The five largest had almost 44 percent of all U.S. bank deposits, up from 37 percent in 2007. A decade before they had just 38 percent. The biggest banks keep getting bigger because they can borrow more cheaply than smaller banks. That's because investors believe the government will bail them out if they get into trouble, rather than force them into a form of bankruptcy.

But if it was in the public's interest to break up giant oil companies and railroads a century ago, and years ago the mammoth telephone company AT&T, it was not unreasonable to break up the extensive tangles of Citigroup, Bank of America, JPMorgan Chase, Goldman Sachs, and Morgan Stanley. There was no clear reason why such large-scale banks were crucial to the U.S. economy or to the living standards of most Americans. Logic and experience would suggest the reverse.

Why didn't politicians do more? It may have had to do with Wall Street's money. The Street is where the money is, and money buys campaign commercials on television. It is difficult to hold people accountable for bad behavior while simultaneously asking them for money. In recent years Wall Street firms and their executives have been uniquely generous to both political parties, emerging as one of the largest benefactors of the Democratic Party. Between November 2008 and November 2009, Wall Street firms and executives doled out $42 million to lawmakers, mostly to members of the House and Senate banking committees and House and Senate leaders. Wall Street doled out $28 million in the presidential election of 2012, dwarfing the contributions of most other industries.

Any potential government toughness with regard to the Street was also constrained by the revolving door of people moving between Wall Street, top jobs at the Treasury Department, and banking committees of the Senate and House. Deep wellsprings of empathy are commonly found in the troughs of anticipated employment.

Had the banks not been rescued from their wildly irresponsible bets, several would have disappeared just like Lehman Brothers. Yet less than a year later they were back at it, confident they would be bailed out by taxpayers if their new bets went sour. And they were using a portion of their winnings to essentially bribe lawmakers to keep the game going, much as it had been before. Who could blame the public for believing the game was fixed?

Wall Street has not been the only beneficiary of the fidelity of lobbyists and the acute responsiveness of Congress to the wealthy. According to the Center for Responsive Politics, spending on lobbyists escalated from $1.44 billion in 1998 to $3.47 billion in 2009, and almost all of these lobbyists represented big corporations and their executives. Even these figures understate the true extent, because lobbying laws are vague about who must register as a lobbyist, and enforcement is casual at best. The numbers also fail to reflect myriad meetings between lawmakers and the corporate executives and other wealthy people who bankroll campaigns.

Sad to say, as the costs of campaigns have escalated, political contributions from wealthy individuals have grown steadily more important. (To be sure, the Internet has created more opportunities for small donors to participate, but large donors continue to dominate.) Even before the Supreme Court's grotesque 2010 decision in *Citizens United v. Federal Election Commission,* which opened wide the floodgates of corporate money by deeming corporations "people" with First Amendment rights, attempts to reform campaign finance had left wide loopholes. The finance committees of most politicians have become the exclusive domains of the wealthy because only they have networks of affluent friends and business associates who can so readily and efficiently be tapped.

Modern Washington is far removed from that of the Gilded Age at the end of the nineteenth century and start of the twentieth, when, it's been said, the lackeys of robber barons literally deposited sacks of cash on the desks of friendly legislators. Today's culture of political corruption rarely takes the form of outright bribes or campaign contributions expressly linked to particular votes. A wealthy Wall Street or corporate executive receives an invitation to have coffee with, say, the chairman of an important congressional committee. The invitation may have come about without any effort on the part of the executive, or he may have solicited it. In either case, the real value of the event to the executive is that it confirms to others that he is capable of commanding the attention of a powerful person in Washington. The photograph memorializing the coffee chat, complete with signature, hangs discreetly on the executive's office wall. The personal thank-you note that arrived from the politician is slyly shared with others.

What this does for the executive is incalculable. He has become someone with access to a powerful ear—become a person, it is presumed, with connections, a person with influence. Such a reputation is valuable to him socially; even more so financially. It gives the people with whom he does business the sense that he can deliver on whatever he proposes. It doesn't matter if this inference is incorrect. The appearance of power means that from now on the executive's clients, customers, suppliers, creditors, and investors will be that much more willing to cut a deal.

In return, the politician may or may not get a campaign contribution from the wealthy executive. But as far as the politician is concerned, that donation is not the point of the transaction. Through the executive, the politician gains access to a network of wealthy people: the executive's friends, business partners, and colleagues, and members of his club or board. When the occasion arises, the wealthy executive introduces them to the politician. Then come their own invitations to breakfast, coffee, dinner, golf. In time, the new acquaintances will give money, and also ask that others do so.

No policy has been altered, no bill or vote willfully changed. But inevitably, as the politician enters into these endless social rounds among the networks of the wealthy, his view of the world is affected. Increasingly, the politician hears the same kinds of suggestions, the same concerns and priorities. The wealthy do not speak in one voice, to be sure, but they share a broad common perspective. The politician hears only indirectly and abstractly from the less comfortable members of society. They are not at the coffees and the dinners. They do not tell him directly and repeatedly, in casual banter and through personal stories, how they view the world. They do not speak continuously into the politician's ear about *their* concerns. The politician learns of those concerns from his pollsters, and from occasional political appearances back in his home district, but he is not immersed in them as he is in the culture of the comfortable. In this way, access to the network of the wealthy does not necessarily buy a politician's vote. It buys his mind.

As lobbying has become more lucrative, an ever larger portion of former federal officials has turned to it. In the 1970s, only about 3 percent of retiring members of Congress went on to become Washington lobbyists. But by 2009 more than 30 percent did, largely because the financial incentives from lobbying had become so large. Starting salaries for well-connected congressional or White House staffers had ballooned to about $500,000. Former chairs of congressional committees and subcommittees commanded $2 million or more to influence legislation in their former committees. According to the Center for Public Integrity, between 1998 and 2004 (years picked because they straddled Democratic and Republican administrations) more than twenty-two hundred former federal officials registered as lobbyists, as did more than two hundred former members of Congress. When Dick Gephardt ran for president in 1988, he said, "I'm running for president because I've had enough of the oil barons, the status-quo apologists, the special-interest lobbyists running amok." By 2009, the former House majority leader was heading up a major Washington lobbying firm that counted among its clients Goldman Sachs, multiple insurance companies, and Peabody Energy, which proclaimed itself the "world's largest private-sector coal company." When Democratic congressman Elijah Cummings threatened to investigate Goldman Sachs, it was Gephardt who ushered Goldman's president to a Capitol Hill meeting. A longtime advocate of universal health care when he was in Congress, by 2009 Gephardt was chairing the Council for American Medical Innovation, a group sponsored by the pharmaceutical industry.

I do not mean to pick on Gephardt, whom I admire for his accomplishments as a dedicated public servant. The point is that a staggering amount of money from big corporations, executives, and other wealthy individuals lies like a thick fog over the nation's capital, enveloping everyone and everything. Not only has it enriched Washington lobbyists, lawyers, and public relations professionals, and seduced thousands of ex-congressmen, but it has also transformed Washington into a glittering city of high-end restaurants and exquisite hotels. It has boosted the price of Washington real estate. Even home prices in its surrounding counties proved remarkably resilient during the Great Recession. Seven of Washington's suburban counties are listed by the Census Bureau as among the nation's twenty with highest per capita incomes.

In order to be enacted, almost all major legislation now requires payoffs to powerful corporations and industries. President Obama felt it necessary to guarantee the executives of big health insurers and pharmaceutical manufacturers that they'd come out ahead—with tens of millions of new customers, along with generous federal subsidies—lest these powerful moneyed interests use their clout to kill his proposed health care legislation, as they had Bill Clinton's. Yet this payoff would necessarily mean higher health care costs for middle-class Americans. Similarly, in order to get off first base with legislation to cap greenhouse gases and allow companies to trade permits to pollute within the cap, Congress had to promise generous subsidies for the nuclear industry and big agribusiness's ethanol, and for the development of so-called clean coal. (Wall Street was supportive, one expects, because the Street would collect billions of dollars on the "trade" part of cap-and-trade, and the market for trading permits would include derivatives and be open to speculators.) Here again, the middle class would be left with much of the tab.

A middle class devoid of coping mechanisms, feeling poorer and more vulnerable than before, is bound to be more sensitive to what has become a commonplace occurrence: government's advancing the interests of large American companies—using taxpayer dollars to subsidize their basic research and development, opening foreign markets to them, giving them lucrative government contracts—thereby raising their share prices. This richly awards their executives and dominant shareholders. Yet these same companies outsource more and more of their production abroad, leaving behind American workers with fewer jobs and lower pay.

The distressed middle class is also likely to take more notice of the regressive direction of tax policy. Although Democrats raise taxes on the rich more readily than Republicans do, they provide generous exceptions. In 2001, President George W. Bush gutted the estate tax by dramatically increasing the amount of money that could be passed on to heirs tax free (from $1 million in 2001 to $3.5 million by 2009, or $7 million per couple), and then scheduling its repeal in 2010. But rather than restore the tax and return the exemption to $1 million, the Obama administration, abetted by congressional Democrats, agreed to allow wealthy couples to transfer to their children up to $10 million tax free. Only the richest 2,000 American families benefit from this change, but it is expensive. Between 2012 and 2021, it will drain $544 billion from the federal treasury.

Another glaring example: Some hedge-fund managers and most private-equity fund managers (who often take home tens of millions of dollars) pay only slightly more than 15 percent of their income in taxes each year—a lower rate than that paid by many middle-income Americans earning barely a tiny fraction of such incomes. This bizarre disparity is the result of an obsolete tax loophole allowing certain money managers to treat their hefty fees as long-term capital gains rather than as ordinary income. Even after repeated attempts by the administration and House Democrats to close the loophole, Senate Democrats and Republicans joined forces to preserve most of it. The reason was their dependence on the hedge-fund and equity-fund managers for generous campaign donations.

Meanwhile, starved of revenues, state and local governments have been increasing sales taxes. Such taxes fall disproportionately on the middle class and the poor, who devote a larger portion of their incomes to purchases than do the wealthy. (Astonishingly, some Washington politicians and pundits are pushing what amounts to a *national* sales tax to replace the federal income tax.) At the same time, local governments are relying to an ever greater extent on property taxes, which fall disproportionately on middle-class taxpayers, who have most of their assets in their homes, rather than on the wealthy, whose assets are mainly in financial instruments.

A tilted playing field might be tolerable if Americans felt they could get ahead eventually nonetheless. But as I pointed out earlier, access to a good education has become the prerequisite to top-paying positions (and to valuable networks of well-connected friends and parents), and the wealthy's increased lock on excellent schools and colleges has stacked the deck in favor of their children. Once, America was a place of rapid social mobility where anyone could get ahead. Now, many of the children of the middle class attend public primary and secondary schools that are falling behind, or make their way to public universities whose funding has been slashed, as states are forced to trim budgets.

Perhaps the most convincing evidence that the game is rigged is the deafening silence about all this. You would think political leaders would talk about the nation's surging inequality and the flattening of middle-class incomes. But as the divergence in income and wealth has grown to stunning proportions, it is rare to find even a Democratic politician who dwells on it.

As a result, some Americans already have moved from distrust to anger. Given the intransigence of high unemployment and the near certainty of lower real wages for a large portion of Americans, it seems likely that more will join them in the years ahead. And because politics abhors a vacuum almost as much as nature does, the Independence Party, or something like it, could be expected to fill the void—bringing with it nationalism, isolationism, intolerance, and paranoia. Unless, that is, there is an alternative.

7

The Politics of Anger

There is an old Russian story about a suffering peasant whose neighbor is rich and well connected. In time, the rich neighbor obtains a cow, something the peasant could never afford. The peasant prays to God for help. When God asks the peasant what he wants God to do, the peasant replies, "Kill the cow."

In Russia, the game was often rigged, and peasant uprisings were more commonly directed at bringing down the rich than at bringing everyone else up. Unless present trends are reversed, we could find ourselves in a similar position. The Independence Party or its facsimile will kill the cow.

Social psychology has shown that people gain almost as much satisfaction from reducing the winnings of those who seem to have gotten them unfairly as from receiving a modest portion of such winnings for themselves. For years I've conducted a simple experiment in my classes that proves the point. I ask my students to join with the person sitting next to them to form a two-person team. I then announce that I'm going to give one member of the team a simulated thousand dollar bill, and will ask that person to write down on a piece of paper how much of it will be shared with his teammate, and then silently pass the paper over. I make it very clear to both that unless the teammate accepts the offer, neither of them will receive anything.

Some recipients willingly accept a small amount, as little as $1. After all, they reason, they're better off than they were before, regardless of how much their teammate has ended up with. But most of my students on the receiving end refuse anything short of $250, and a surprising number refuse any offer less than $500. They'd rather end up with nothing—sacrificing quite a lot—than have their teammate "get away with" far more.

Are such students being vindictive? Are they allowing feelings of envy and spite to get in the way of rational thinking? When I ask them why they're willing to sacrifice so much, they often say it's worth it to them in order to avoid what they consider to be an unfair outcome and disrespectful treatment.

It is no great leap from my simple classroom exercise to a national movement. Americans who would slash trade and investment with other nations, for example, might fully understand that this would deny all Americans access to cheaper goods from abroad. Yet they might still support such a move if they believed it would cause people at the top even greater loss. Likewise, they'd support confiscatory taxes on the wealthy, even understanding that such rates will discourage investment and thereby hurt everyone, because such taxes would hurt the rich most of all. They would get behind all sorts of policies that slowed the economy and reduced efficiencies if those at the top would lose out to a greater extent than they did. In short, they'd opt to kill the cow.

Economic anger could be detected in March 2009 when, after the government bailed out AIG with over $150 billion, the firm awarded its top executives $165 million in "retention bonuses" and a $440,000 spa retreat at the St. Regis resort. Angry citizens traveled by bus to the estates of AIG executives to tell them exactly what they thought. Others wrote threatening letters and e-mails. AIG executives were forced to hire private security guards to protect themselves and their families. One, nicknamed "Jackpot Jimmy" by a New York City tabloid, complained, "I feel horrible. This has been a complete invasion of privacy. You have to understand, there are kids involved, there have been death threats."

Such resentments have also come to the surface as voters penalize politicians too closely identified with the financial industry. In May 2010, Utah's GOP refused to support the reelection of conservative senator Robert Bennett because of his vote in favor of the Wall Street bailout. In November 2009, New Jersey governor Jon Corzine lost his reelection bid despite spending a substantial fortune on his campaign; pundits assigned part of the blame to his being a former head of Goldman Sachs. In 2010, Connecticut senator Chris Dodd did not run for reelection in part due to voters' disquiet over his history of cozy relations with the financial industry. Other politicians have paid the price of appearing to be privileged insiders. Former Senate Democratic minority leader Tom Daschle had to withdraw his name from nomination for Obama's cabinet because after leaving the Senate he became a wealthy consultant to lobbyists and had profited handsomely from his connections and failed to pay taxes he owed. New York City's mayor Michael Bloomberg won a surprisingly narrow reelection in the fall of 2009 despite his creditable record and sizable campaign spending. Voters, it seemed, were turned off by his vast wealth and his willingness to spend it on the campaign. (Just prior to the election, *New York* magazine blared in a headline: MICHAEL BLOOMBERG IS ABOUT TO BUY HIMSELF A THIRD TERM.)

The stirrings of backlash can also be seen in Americans' sharp turn against international trade. In a poll taken in December 2009 by the Pew Research Center, only 43 percent of Americans thought trade agreements benefited the U.S. economy, and a growing percentage wanted the U.S. out of international bodies such as the International Trade Commission. Meanwhile, mounting resentments toward immigrants were evident across the land. In 2010, Arizona authorized police to demand proof of citizenship from anyone they had a "reasonable suspicion" was undocumented—in effect, inviting them to stop Latinos—and by 2011 similar efforts were under way in at least a half dozen other states. State legislators also sought to bar illegal immigrants from public colleges, and to prevent their American-born children from becoming American citizens.

Economic resentments lay behind the public's growing suspicions of the Federal Reserve Board and its chairman. In early 2010, reflecting that backlash, the Senate nearly blocked Ben Bernanke's confirmation to a second term. Members of Congress from both parties pushed legislation to make the Fed's actions more transparent and open to political scrutiny. Bond traders on Wall Street feared the Fed's independence would be compromised.

The shrillest part of the backlash could be heard in the increasing bitterness and virulence of the nation's politics. During congressional recesses, senators and representatives have been harassed by voters at town meetings that have turned into shouting matches and occasionally become violent; self-described "Tea Partiers" have derided "establishment" Republicans and threatened them with electoral defeat. In February 2010, at the Conservative Political Action Conference, Governor Tim Pawlenty of Minnesota attacked "the elites" who believe Tea Partiers are "not as sophisticated because a lot of them didn't go to Ivy League Schools" and "don't hang out at . . . Chablis-drinking, Brie-eating parties in San Francisco." After his son Rand

Paul was selected for Kentucky's Senate seat in May 2010, Congressman Ron Paul explained that voters wanted to "get rid of the power people who run the show, the people who think they're above everybody else." In April 2012, Representative Alan West, a Florida Republican, asserted there were "78 to 81" Democrats in Congress who were members of the Communist party.

By 2012, it was difficult to find any unifying principle behind the Tea Party other than the same hostility toward government, big business, and Wall Street shared by much of the rest of the public. Surveys showed that people who described themselves as members or supporters of the Tea Party tended to be white, Republican, male, and wealthier than most other Americans. And where most Republicans described themselves as "dissatisfied" with Washington, Tea Partiers were more likely to say they were "angry." Yet a large number of Democrats also claimed to be angry. And by the end of 2010, almost two-thirds of Americans told pollsters the nation was heading in the wrong direction.

Talk radio and yell television emit escalating vitriol as they channel the "mad as hell" ire of many Americans. The ire has been directed at a variety of targets: immigrants, African Americans, the poor, foreigners, "East Coast elites," "San Francisco elites," "intellectuals," Democratic politicians, Republican politicians, corporate leaders, Wall Street executives. Even I've been on the receiving end. In 2012, Bill O'Reilly, the outsized personality of Fox News, said on his show "Robert Reich is a communist who secretly adores Karl Marx." (I'm not, and I don't.) The blogosphere has became a cauldron of insult and rage.

While the right has railed at big government and the left has fulminated against big business and Wall Street, there is a widening overlap. "The wizards in Washington and on Wall Street have us figured out," says Chuck Baldwin, as quoted in the Pocatello Tea Party's online newsletter. "Along with their compatriots in the propaganda press corps, they know that no matter how loudly we scream, how much we protest, or how angry we become, the system is rigged to protect them." It was the bailout of Wall Street that really "got this ball rolling," says Joseph Farah, publisher of WorldNetDaily, a Web site popular among Tea Party adherents. "That's where the anger, where the frustration took root." At the Utah state convention that unseated Robert Bennett, the mob repeatedly shouted, "TARP! TARP! TARP!"

Historian Richard Hofstadter once wrote a famous essay about the recurring strain of, as he put it, a "paranoid style in American politics"—an underlying readiness among average voters to see conspiracies among powerful elites supposedly plotting against them. The paranoia rises during periods of economic stress. It animated the pre–Civil War Know-Nothings and Anti-Masonic movements, the populist agitators of the late nineteenth century, the Ku Klux Klan, and the John Birch Society (whose founder, Robert Welch, accused Dwight Eisenhower of being "a dedicated, conscious agent of the Communist conspiracy"). Some of the current and pending backlash is rooted in a similar paranoia.

Yet for all its bitterness, America's backlash is still tame in comparison to uprisings elsewhere around the globe. During foreign meetings of the G-20 and other global institutions, demonstrators abroad have repeatedly blocked streets and disrupted proceedings. In October 2009, on the sixtieth anniversary of China's communist revolution supposedly designed to create a "classless utopia," that nation was gripped by a wave of anger against its new wealthy elite. A new phrase—"fen fu"—was coined, meaning "to hate the rich."

Economic resentments have not yet propelled anyone into the

White House (unless you count Andrew Jackson's 1828 victory, including his attack on the Second Bank of the United States and the "elite circle" of business leaders who, he charged, benefited from it at the expense of America's farmers and laborers). At the end of the nineteenth century, America's most famous economic populist was William Jennings Bryan, who won the Democratic nomination for president in 1896 demanding "free coinage of silver." The nation's adherence to the gold standard had caused the dollar to deflate, thereby crushing the nation's farmers, laborers, and other debtors with high payments they hadn't bargained for. A silver standard would have had the reverse effect, causing the dollar to inflate and shrinking their debts. Their enemies were eastern bankers who held most of that debt and naturally favored the gold standard. Bryan took on the bankers, "the few financial magnates who, in a back room, corner the money of the world." In one of the most famously incendiary speeches in American history, he thundered to the assembled delegates, "We shall answer their demands for a gold standard by saying to them, you shall not press down upon the brow of labor this crown of thorns. You shall not crucify mankind upon a cross of gold!" The convention roared its approval, but Bryan lost the election to William McKinley nonetheless. (Perhaps not incidentally, McKinley's campaign manager, Mark Hanna, had raised an unprecedented $3.5 million from big business and plowed most of it into advertising; historians credit Hanna with inventing the modern presidential campaign.)

Before economic stresses and resentments have risen too far, America has traditionally opted for reform. Progressive state legislatures preempted Bryan's prairie populism by enacting a welter of reforms on behalf of farmers and laborers. Theodore Roosevelt stole some of Bryan's thunder by fighting the trusts. Years later, in the depths of the Great Depression, Father Charles Coughlin of Detroit, known as the "radio priest" for his weekly political broadcast, repeatedly chastised bankers and financiers—the "debt merchants" and "ventriloquists of Wall Street"—and he inveighed against the Fed, "a system owned by a group of your masters and not by the American people." Coughlin demanded a radical inflation of the currency, which he insisted would redistribute wealth. About the same time, Senator Huey "the Kingfish" Long of Louisiana attacked "imperialistic banking control" and big corporations, and pushed for a tax on corporate assets that would guarantee everyone a minimal income and make "every man a king." Here again, though, reformers preempted the populists. New Deal measures took much of the wind out of Coughlin's and Long's sails. When Coughlin and others joined in a third-party presidential challenge to FDR in 1936, they received around 2 percent of the vote.

During the 1992 presidential election, when the nation was still mired in recession, maverick presidential candidate Ross Perot railed against government deficits, alleging that they hurt average working people. Although Perot's third party never garnered enough votes to get near the Oval Office, five years later Bill Clinton signed the Balanced Budget Act, and soon thereafter balanced the budget. Pat Buchanan, the former Nixon speechwriter who coined the phrase "the silent majority," ran in some Republican primaries on a platform calling for restrictions on immigration, multiculturalism, and gay rights. Buchanan garnered 3 million votes, hardly enough to displace George Bush. He tried again in 1996, charging that members of America's establishment "hear the shouts of the peasants from over the hill. . . . All the peasants are coming with pitchforks." It was a memorable phrase, but it didn't get Buchanan any farther. By then, a strong economic recovery had becalmed Buchanan's pitchforked peasants. In 2000, Ralph Nader ran for president as the Green Party candidate, assailing the power of "greedy" and "rapacious" corporations. He lost, of course, but some believe he got enough support to tip Florida, and therefore the electoral college and the presidency, to George W. Bush.

To be sure, prolonged economic stress could open the door to demagogues who prey on public anxieties in order to gain power. A classic sociological study of thirty-five dictatorships found that when people feel economically threatened and unhinged from their normal habits, they look to authority figures who promise simple remedies proffering scapegoats. Adolf Hitler, coming to power only weeks before Roosevelt, gave voice to the phenomenon: "That is the mightiest mission of our Movement, namely, to give the searching and bewildered masses a new, firm belief, a belief which will not abandon them in these days of chaos, which they will swear and abide by, so that at least somewhere they will again find a place where their hearts can be at rest."

Americans are not immune to this temptation, but we have not yet succumbed. Just before Franklin Roosevelt's inauguration, as the nation fell into the depths of the Great Depression, some influential Americans thought the nation needed a dictator. The famed syndicated columnist Walter Lippmann advocated a "mild species of dictatorship" that would "help us over the roughest spots in the road ahead." Some of Roosevelt's closest advisors warned him that unless he assumed dictatorial power, the country would face revolution. The revolution never happened; nor did the dictatorship.

This is not to argue that reform in America will inevitably preempt demagoguery or bitter "kill the cow" populism. So far our political system has shown a knack for stopping backlashes before they get too far out of hand. The question is whether reform will come this time, on a scale that's needed. By the time Margaret Jones and her Independence Party (or whatever other form the backlash might take) take control, it will be too late.

PART III

The Bargain Restored

1

What Should Be Done:
A New Deal for the Middle Class

I could have grounded my argument in morality: It is simply unfair for a handful of Americans to take home such a large share of total income when so many others are struggling to make ends meet. Or I could have based it on traditional American values: Such a lopsided distribution is at odds with the nation's history and its ideal of equal opportunity—especially when the deck seems stacked in favor of those at the top. I could have talked about how this degree of inequality undermines the nation's moral authority and its standing in the world.

I have chosen instead to base my argument on two tangible threats that such inequality poses to everyone—including even the wealthiest and most influential among us. One is economic: Unless America's middle class receives a fair share, it cannot consume nearly what the nation is capable of producing, at least without going deeply into debt. And debt on this scale is unsustainable, as we have seen. The inevitable result is slower economic growth and an economy increasingly susceptible to great booms and terrible busts. The other threat is political: Widening inequality, coupled with a growing perception that big business and Wall Street are in cahoots with big government for the purpose of making the rich even richer, gives fodder to demagogues on the extreme right and the extreme left. They gain power by turning the public's economic anxieties into resentments against particular people and groups. Isolationist and nativist, often racist, and willing to sacrifice overall prosperity for the sake of achieving their ends, such demagogues and the movements they inspire can cause great harm.

As I've shown, the Great Recession has accelerated both troubling trends. With the bursting of the housing bubble, many middle-class homeowners who can no longer use their homes as piggy banks must face the reality of flat or declining wages. The downturn also has forced—or given a ready excuse for—firms to increase profits by shrinking their payrolls, laying off millions of workers and reducing the pay of millions more. It has simultaneously induced firms to ratchet up the pay of their "talent"—the executives and traders who drive the profits. At the same time, big business and Wall Street have been able to enhance their profits by exacting money and other favors from government—even from one under the nominal control of the Democratic Party.

Unless these trends are reversed, the financially stressed middle class will not have the purchasing power to keep the economy growing. This will hurt even those who are well-off. A political backlash could generate a similar result, or worse. Margaret Jones and her Independence Party are fictional, but the anger on which she bases her appeal is not.

I cannot pretend that the following measures would remedy these problems altogether, but they represent important steps. They would help restore the basic bargain. As such, they would fill the gap in aggregate demand, and would preempt a politics of resentment. Some of these reforms would be costly, but I suggest ways to pay for them so they would not increase the national debt. To the contrary, they are likely to produce a budget surplus. And because they would generate stronger and more sustainable growth than the policies we now have, they would shrink the debt as a proportion of the national economy in years to come. The costs of inaction are far greater. An economy functioning well below its capacity is a terrible waste of all our resources, especially of our people; a society riven by resentment is potentially unstable.

A reverse income tax. The most immediate way to reestablish shared prosperity is through a "reverse income tax" that supplements the wages of the middle class. Instead of money being withheld from their paychecks to pay taxes to the government, money would be added to their paychecks by the government.

A similar idea was proposed by the prizewinning economist Milton Friedman, and we now provide this for low-income workers through the Earned Income Tax Credit. The EITC has not only helped reduce poverty but has also increased the incomes of families most likely to spend that additional money, and thereby create more jobs. In 2009, the EITC was the nation's largest anti-poverty program. Over 24 million households received wage supplements. Given what's happened to middle-class incomes, the EITC should be expanded and extended upward.

Under my plan, full-time workers earning $20,000 or less (this and all subsequent outlays are in 2009 dollars) would receive a wage supplement of $15,000. This supplement would decline incrementally up the income scale, to $10,000 for full-time workers earning $30,000; to $5,000 for full-time workers earning $40,000; and then to zero for full-time workers earning $50,000.

The tax rate for full-time workers with incomes between $50,000 and $90,000—whether the source of those incomes are wages, salaries, or capital gains—would be cut to 10 percent of earnings. The taxes for people with incomes of between $90,000 and $160,000 would be 20 percent, whatever the income source.

The yearly cost to the federal government of these wage supplements would be $633 billion. The cost of the tax cuts for middle-income families would be billions more. But these lost revenues would be replaced by the following two initiatives: a carbon tax, and higher taxes on the top 5 percent of incomes.

A carbon tax. We should tax fossil fuels (coal, oil, and gas), based on how many tons of carbon dioxide such fuels contain. The tax would be collected at the mine or port of entry for each fossil fuel, and would gradually rise over time in order to push energy companies and users to spew less carbon into the atmosphere. (A yearly auction for the "right" to pollute under a certain maximum cap that tightened year by year would theoretically have the same effect and generate about the same amount of money—but only if permits were not handed out to politically powerful polluters free of charge or exchanged for imaginary and unverifiable "offsets" that a company might claim by, say, planting trees in Brazil.)

If initially set at $35 per metric ton of carbon dioxide or its equivalent, such a tax would raise over $210 billion in its first year alone. By the time it reached $115 per ton, it would yield about $600 billion per year. The public wouldn't pay this tax directly, but indirectly as the prices of goods rose in proportion to how much carbon was used in their production. For example, a tax of $115 per ton would add about $1 to the price of a gallon of gasoline and 6¢ per kilowatt-hour to the price of electricity.

If the revenues from the carbon tax went into wage supplements, middle- and lower-income Americans would still come out far ahead. A carbon tax would have two additional advantages. First, it would push energy companies and businesses to invest in new ways to reduce greenhouse gases, and in lower-carbon fuels and products; it could thereby lead to the development of cheaper and more efficient sources of energy. Second, by stimulating such investments, the carbon tax would also boost aggregate demand.

Higher marginal tax rates on the wealthy. In a nation facing a widening chasm between the very rich and everyone else, it is not unreasonable to expect those at the top to pay a higher tax on their incomes, from whatever source (wages, salaries, or capital gains). I propose that people in the top 1 percent, with incomes of more than $410,000, pay a marginal tax of 55 percent; those in the top 2 percent, earning over $260,000, pay a marginal tax of 50 percent; and those earning over $160,000, roughly the top 5 percent, pay 40 percent. These taxes, when added to the modest amounts contributed by taxpayers who earn between $50,000 and $160,000 under my plan, would raise $600 billion more than our current tax system per year. Added to the $210 billion generated by the carbon tax just in its first year, the total new revenues would be $810 billion initially and would increase as carbon tax revenues increased. These would more than pay for the income supplements and tax cuts I propose. I would use the surplus for additional initiatives listed in the following pages that require funding, and for reducing the federal deficit.

Under my proposal, income from capital gains would be treated no differently from income derived from wages and salaries. Someone with a total income of between $50,000 and $90,000 would pay 10 percent, even if a majority of that income is from capital gains. That is substantially less than the 15 percent tax rate on capital gains today. By the same token, someone with a total income of several million dollars would pay a marginal tax of 55 percent on all income, regardless of how much of it came from capital gains. (The four hundred highest-income taxpayers in 2007, each with an average income of over $300 million, paid only 17 percent of their total incomes in taxes that year, because most of their incomes were treated as capital gains. This makes a mockery of the ideal of a progressive tax system.)

Furthermore, these tax rates are not out of line with most of our history over the last century, during which time the nation's productivity and overall economy grew quickly. As noted, from 1936 to 1980, the top marginal tax rate was 70 percent or more. Since 1987, the official top rate has remained below 40 percent, and the effective rate, after all deductions and credits, between 20 percent and 25 percent. Yet higher taxes on top earners have not correlated with slower growth, the claims of so-called supply-side economists to the contrary notwithstanding. During the almost three decades spanning 1951 to 1980, when the top rate was between 70 percent and 92 percent, average annual growth in the American economy was 3.7 percent. Between 1983 and the start of the Great Recession, when the top rate ranged between 35 percent and 39 percent, average growth was 3 percent.

So-called supply-siders are fond of claiming that Ronald Reagan's 1981 tax cuts caused the 1980s economic boom. There is no evidence to support their claim. In fact, that boom followed Reagan's 1982 tax *increase*. The 1990s boom likewise was not the result of a tax cut; most of it followed Bill Clinton's 1993 tax increase.

My proposal is not a Robin Hood–like redistribution. The wage supplements and tax reductions I'm proposing for the middle class would enable them to spend more, and their spending would help move the economy to full capacity and sustained growth. Consequently, companies would enjoy higher profits, and the stock market would rise. Although the rich would pay higher taxes and thereby receive a somewhat smaller share of the economy's overall gains, those overall gains would be much larger than they would be otherwise. Hence, richer Americans are very likely to come out ahead compared to where they were before—as they did during the Great Prosperity, when they paid substantially higher taxes but enjoyed the fruits of faster growth.

A reemployment system rather than an unemployment system. The old unemployment insurance system was designed to tide people over until they got their jobs back at the end of a downturn. Nowadays, most job losers never get their jobs back, and the ranks of the long-term unemployed are extraordinarily high. People who are unemployed for long periods have difficulty getting back into the job market, and they drain family assets. High levels of long-term unemployed strain our social safety nets. What's needed is a *reemployment* system that speeds and smoothes the way for those who become unemployed to find new jobs.

One piece of such a reemployment system would be wage insurance. Any job loser who takes a new job that pays less than his or her former job would be eligible for 90 percent of the difference, for up to two years. After two years, many workers would have acquired enough on-the-job training to render them sufficiently productive to warrant wages nearly as high as the wages they formerly had on the job they lost. Wage insurance would speed the movement of laid-off workers into new jobs because it would induce them to take jobs that pay less rather than wait for ones that pay as much as the job that was lost. It would thereby save the costs of unemployment benefits and would generate added revenues as reemployed workers pay income taxes earlier than otherwise.

For workers who need additional skills, income support of 90 percent of the former wages would be provided for up to a year while a worker is engaged full-time in approved training or education programs. Longer-term training has been shown to be more effective than short-term, especially when it gives people the basic tools they need to continue learning on the job. If job seekers choose to enroll in programs that prepare them for fields in which labor is likely to be in short supply, such as nursing or teaching, they would receive income support for an additional year of training and education. As participants acquire the kinds of skills that are rewarded in the new economy and fill positions for which there are labor shortages, we could all expect to reap the benefits of this program in the longer term through stronger economic growth, higher tax revenues, and less dependence on social safety nets.

I estimate the total new costs of a reemployment system to be $3 billion a year over and above the $2.35 billion that the federal government now spends on unemployment insurance in an average year. In time, however, the costs of the reemployment system would drop as the skills of the labor force improved and the rate of long-term unemployment declined.

Any remaining shortfall in revenues to cover this program would be made up by a severance tax on profitable corporations that lay off their workers. Under the current system, employers do not pay the social costs of layoffs—including additional unemployment benefits and the extra needs of families in distress. It stands to reason that companies would be less inclined toward layoffs if they had to pay these costs. What is needed is a one-time severance tax on any layoff equal to 75 percent of the full cost of the laid-off worker's yearly salary, for all workers under the median wage, and 50 percent for all workers above it, up to 200 percent of the median. Such a tax would not only give employers more incentive to keep workers on, but would also help pay for the wage insurance and skill upgrades of the reemployment system.

. . .

School vouchers based on family income. Over the longer term, the best way to boost the earnings of Americans in the bottom half is to improve their education and skills. To that end, spending on public schools should be replaced by vouchers in amounts inversely related to family income that families can cash in at any school meeting certain minimum standards. For example, the $8,000 now spent per child in a particular state would be turned into $14,000 education vouchers for each school-age child in a poor family, and $2,000 vouchers for each child in a very wealthy family.

School vouchers in this progressive form would improve overall school performance by introducing competition into the school system. They would also give lower- and middle-income families more purchasing power in the education market. Schools located in neighborhoods where there are many lower-income families would get immediate infusions of billions of dollars to upgrade their physical plants, buy new textbooks, and hire more and better teachers. Yet under my proposal, such schools would not be able to count on these extra revenues forever. After an initial three years, they would have to compete with other schools that might put those sizable vouchers to even better uses. Some competitors would be organized as independent, nonprofit "charter" schools. Others would be public schools located nearby in adjoining school districts or communities.

I would also expect wealthy suburban school districts to compete vigorously for lower- and middle-income children and the generous vouchers they would bring. These upscale districts would need the money in order to make ends meet; they couldn't possibly meet their expenses at $2,000 per student. They would even have a financial incentive to arrange vans to transport the children from poorer neighborhoods.

Progressive vouchers should also be made available to families to support early childhood education, providing stimulating care for all children from infancy until they are ready to enter first grade. Few other educational expenditures have so uniformly and consistently shown such positive results. Children in these programs are more likely to graduate from high school, attend college, and be fully employed when adults than are children who have not participated. Children in these programs have been shown to earn more, commit less crime, and experience less teenage pregnancy. A total of $20 billion per year should be devoted to early childhood education. This money would come from the reverse income tax.

College loans linked to subsequent earnings. A large and growing percentage of college students from lower- and middle-income families must finance their education with student loans. This discourages some students from pursuing higher education for fear they won't be able to get jobs that pay enough. In 2009, about two-thirds of incoming college students expressed concern about their ability to pay for their education. More than half of them had taken out loans. This way of financing higher education imposes an additional burden on students who wish to pursue lower-paying professions like teaching or social work rather than higher-paying professions like business and corporate law. The system thereby robs society of many low-wage professionals whose work is socially useful and desirable.

We need to change the way higher education is financed in America. Tuition should be free at all public colleges and universities. Students who elect to attend a private college or university should be eligible to take out a federal loan. Graduates of public colleges and universities, and borrowers of federal loans, should be required to pay a fixed percentage—say, 10 percent—of their taxable earnings for their first ten years of full-time work into a fund that finances public colleges and universities and provides loans to students attending private colleges and universities. After that, graduates would have no further obligations; loans would be considered fully paid. This way, graduates who pursue low-income occupations such as social work, teaching, or legal services would be subsidized by graduates who pursue high-income occupations including business, finance, and corporate law.

Ten percent is my best estimate, but as long as the payback percentage were set to recoup the full cost of tuition at public universities or the loans for private, the system will not require any additional federal revenues.

Medicare for all. The passage of health care legislation in 2010 represents only the first step toward reform. The next stage should be Medicare for all. The most efficient way to provide all Americans with high-quality health care is to allow everyone to sign up for Medicare and to subsidize the costs for middle-class and lower-income families.

It will become apparent that the 2010 reform cannot adequately contain soaring health care costs. Health care premiums, deductibles, and co-payments will continue to eat up more and more of the paychecks of the middle class. Americans spend more on health care per person than any other nation in the world, and costs are rising faster than inflation. Yet we have the highest infant mortality of all the world's advanced industrialized nations, and life expectancy in the United States is shorter than in forty other nations, including Jordan and the Cayman Islands. We are the only wealthy nation that does not ensure that all citizens have coverage; as of 2010, some 45 million people were without insurance.

The main reason for the soaring costs and poor results is the way our system is organized. We are the only advanced nation whose citizens largely depend on private, for-profit insurers. The result is complicated, expensive, and inequitable. A study by the Harvard Medical School and the Canadian Institute for Health Information shows that over 30 percent of U.S. health care spending—more than $1,000 per person each year—goes for administrative costs. This is nearly twice the percentage of administrative costs in Canada. Medicare's administrative costs (in the range of 3 percent) are well below such costs of large companies that self-insure (5 to 10 percent of premiums), companies in the small-group market (25 to 27 percent of premiums), and individual insurance (40 percent). In a more "apples to apples" comparison, the Congressional Budget Office has found that administrative costs under Medicare are less than 2 percent of expenditures, compared with 11 percent for private plans under Medicare Advantage, the private-insurance option under Medicare. Allowing Medicare to use its bargaining power with drug companies and health care providers would bring down medical costs even further. Estimates of how much would be saved by extending Medicare to cover the entire population range from $58 billion to $400 billion a year, enough to subsidize coverage for many if not all Americans who need it and constrain the costs of co-payments and premiums for everyone else, without busting the federal budget or imposing higher taxes.

Making Medicare available to all Americans is not a very large step when you consider that by 2010, even before the new legislation was implemented, almost half of Americans received some form of public health care (older Americans through Medicare; poorer Americans through Medicaid and the Children's Health Insurance Program; veterans through the Veterans Health Administration; government workers as well as members of Congress through a health plan open to federal employees). Nor is it a pie-in-the-sky idea politically. I believe most Americans would support it. They supported the so-called public option. In a poll conducted for NBC News and *The Wall Street Journal* in June 2009, 76 percent of Americans said it was either "extremely" or "quite" important to "give people a choice of both a public plan administered by the federal government and a private plan for their health insurance." Once the 2010 health bill is implemented and its costs become apparent, the public will be readier to support Medicare for all.

Public goods. There should be a sizable increase in public goods such as public transportation, public parks and recreational facilities, and public museums and libraries. And they should be free of charge to users (the trend in recent years toward "user fees" should be reversed). Such public goods improve the quality of life for many people who cannot afford the equivalent private goods—their own cars, manicured gardens, art collections, books, and health club memberships, for example. In this way, public goods partly make up for stagnant or declining wages.

Public goods typically do not use up lots of scarce resources or cause as much environmental damage as their private equivalents, and they generate jobs and add to overall demand in the economy. Making them free maximizes these societal benefits. For instance, an expanded system of free public transportation, including high-speed rail, would dramatically reduce traffic congestion—estimated to cost Americans more than $85 billion a year in wasted hours and gas—and cut carbon emissions. The benefits are easily worth the cost.

Money out of politics. Finally, and not least, we are all painfully aware of the failures of our democracy. As inequality has widened, money flowing from large corporations, Wall Street, and their executives and traders has increasingly distorted political decision making. We need strong campaign-finance laws, more generous public financing of elections (matching dollar for dollar whatever an opponent raises privately), stricter limits on campaign contributions, and limits on so-called issue advertising, which is partisan advertising under a different name. Recent Supreme Court decisions protect some of these activities as forms of free speech under the First Amendment to the Constitution. Ultimately, these decisions must be overturned.

In the meantime, we should require that all political contributions go through "blind trusts" so that no candidate can ever know who contributed what. Political corruption occurs when officials favor certain parties over others because the favored parties have provided, or are likely to provide, generous campaign donations. The money is the quid pro quo for the political favor. A law requiring that all political contributions go through blind trusts that would maintain the anonymity of donors (with criminal penalties for disclosure) would not prevent any person or group from *claiming* they made or will make a generous donation. It is likely that the number of persons and groups making such claims would increase dramatically, because officials will never be able to check on the veracity of such claims. That is the point. The inability to check will undermine the credibility of all such claims, thereby making it impossible for any person or group to "collect" on their donation by getting favorable treatment. The *quid* would be severed from the *quo*.

2

How It Could Get Done

This is not an unrealistic agenda. It is practical and doable. And given how concentrated income and wealth have become in America, it is commonsensical. It would begin to move the pendulum back toward more shared prosperity.

But to implement it would require cooperation at all levels of society. Though that may seem unlikely now, a major crisis could well unite those at the grass roots who seek positive reform rather than "kill the cow" reactionary politics with the leaders of labor, big business, and Wall Street. Theodore Roosevelt and Woodrow Wilson discovered this in the first decade of the twentieth century as they struggled to implement reforms with the help of progressive organizations at the state and local levels. They were marginally successful, but the economic and political crises of their era were not large enough to compel major reform on the national level. That had to await Franklin D. Roosevelt, who presided over an economic crisis so perilous it hurled the nation toward the New Deal.

Barack Obama discovered much the same phenomenon in the first months of his administration, when the economy teetered on the brink. But with the immediate crisis contained, political support for large-scale reform slackened. Obama might still have succeeded if he had framed the challenge accurately. But in reassuring the public that jobs would return, he missed a key opportunity to expose the longer-term trend and its dangers. By averting the immediate financial crisis and then claiming that the economy was on the mend, he left us with a diffuse set of ongoing economic problems that seemed unrelated and inexplicable—rather like the citizens of a village whose fire chief succeeds in protecting the biggest office buildings but leaves smaller fires simmering all over town. Without a broad understanding of how one problem connects to another, the public can neither see nor react to the overall conflagration. It feels the heat coming from many places—housing foreclosures, continued high unemployment, lower earnings, less economic security, widening inequality, soaring pay on Wall Street and in executive suites—but is bewildered, anxious, and, in many cases, angry.

Legislation to improve America's health care system illustrates the paradox. Initially, the public was strongly supportive. But the president and Democratic leaders failed to link the reform of health care to the long-term economic crisis faced by most Americans, and to a broader agenda of getting the nation back to more widely shared prosperity. As unemployment rose through 2009, the public understandably focused its attention on the losses of jobs and earnings, and threats to their homes and savings. Without a larger framework, fixing health care appeared tangential to these more immediate problems. Consequently, the broad public was not as actively supportive of health care reform as it needed to be in order to weaken the hold of vested interests. As I've pointed out, in order to gain passage, the White House and Democratic leaders brokered deals with Big Pharma and private health insurers, who demanded in return that any so-called reform improve their profitability. The resulting legislation does not adequately control future costs, and it will require that Americans pay more for their health insurance than they would have had the deals not been made.

Much the same occurred with efforts to reform the financial system. The White House and Democratic leaders could have described those efforts as means to overhaul economic institutions that bestow outsized rewards on a relative few, while imposing extraordinary costs and risks on almost everyone else. Instead, they defined the goal narrowly, as reducing risks to the financial system created by particular practices on Wall Street. The solution thereby shriveled to a set of technical fixes for how the Street should conduct its business. Once the worst of the financial crisis seemed to have passed, the public basically lost interest.

In these respects, the Obama administration postponed the day of economic reckoning. Now that middle-class coping mechanisms are exhausted, though, that postponement cannot last for long. Americans need to understand what has happened, and why. And they must understand the real choice ahead.

An aftershock in the form of another deep recession might be enough to spur reform. But a slower aftershock—characterized by several years of high unemployment, languishing or declining wages, and slow growth—may not be enough to upend vested interests "that can too readily hold on to their power and increasingly anachronistic views," as Marriner Eccles described them in the 1920s and early 1930s. A slower aftershock is more likely to unleash a political backlash as, over time, more Americans grow skeptical that established institutions will respond to their needs. Yet even under these circumstances, reform could still be galvanized. The early stirring of backlash may be enough to convince established interests that reform is necessary in order to forestall worse repercussions.

Sooner or later, the chief executives of America's largest corporations and Wall Street banks will become concerned about the lackluster economy. Their firms cannot generate profits, year after year, if the American middle class cannot afford to purchase the products and services these firms offer. None but the most globalized American firms will be able to gain enough from foreign markets to make up for the shortfall at home.

The CEOs will also notice the public's increasing anger. Before, the CEOs would have been largely insulated from it. The anger would not have spilled over into their gated communities, vacation retreats, office parks, and well-secured office towers. But at some point in the not-too-distant future it will spill over. Perhaps the CEOs will experience a growing number of troubling incidents (limousines purposefully scratched, enraged people showing up at their Park Avenue and Wall Street office buildings). The executives will hire more security guards to protect their offices and their homes, but this will not allay their concerns. It will become apparent to many of them, as it did to Eccles after the Crash of 1929, that if they "resisted any change designed to benefit all the people, [they] could be consumed by the poisons of social lag [they] had helped create."

The CEOs will also detect a change of mood in Washington. For years, these CEOs and the executives they supervise have showered politicians with contributions. The contributions have proved to be good investments, generating significant returns in the form of lower taxes and of legislation favoring their companies. Yet in the years to come the contributions will become less potent. Although the Supreme Court has allowed an unlimited amount of corporate political money to influence politics, the CEOs will discover this to be a double-edged sword. Vast corporate expenditures will ignite an even greater backlash as more Americans conclude that big business and Wall Street are exerting ever growing control over politics.

The CEOs will note an increasing number of bills introduced to raise tariffs and reduce trade, and limit global investment. Any such moves could have devastating effects on their firms' bottom lines, as well as on their own incomes. The CEOs will also have to contend with legislative proposals to prevent them from firing employees or outsourcing abroad. Top executives on Wall Street will eventually confront attempts to break up their banks and narrowly constrain their investments. CEOs, executives, traders, hedge-fund managers, and others with high incomes will encounter more bills to cap their earnings and their bonuses, limit their wealth, and impose confiscatory taxes.

If nothing is done to counter present trends, the major fault line in American politics will no longer be between Democrats and Republicans, liberals and conservatives. It will be between the "establishment"—political insiders, power brokers, the heads of American business, Wall Street, and the mainstream media—and an increasingly mad-as-hell populace determined to "take back America" from them. Eventually, the Independence Party, or its equivalent, will prevail.

When they understand where all this is heading, the powerful interests that have so far resisted change are likely to see that the alternative is far worse. They will support reforms that lead us back to a fairer distribution of income, wealth, and opportunity. But the longer they take to come around, the larger and more virulent the backlash they will have to contend with.

As I said at the outset of this book, a virtual pendulum underlies the American political economy. We swing from eras in which the benefits of economic growth are concentrated in fewer hands to those in which the gains are more broadly shared, and then back again. We are approaching the end of one such cycle and the start of the next. The Great Prosperity of 1947 to 1975 was followed by three decades of retrenchment, ending in the Great Recession.

The question is not whether the pendulum will swing back. It surely will. The question is *how* it will swing—whether with reforms that widen the circle of prosperity, or with demagoguery that turns America away from the rest of the world, shrinks the economy, and sets Americans against one another.

My bet is on the former. America has an enormous reservoir of resilience and common sense. Whenever we have faced a palpable crisis—a depression, an enveloping war, a profound threat to our civil liberties—we have put partisan politics and abstract ideology aside and gotten on with what needed to be done. Whenever we have faced the moral urgency of living up to our ideals—to recognize the rights of blacks, women, and the disabled, for example—we have risen to the occasion.

None of us can thrive in a nation divided between a small number of people receiving an ever larger share of the nation's income and wealth, and everyone else receiving a declining share. The lopsidedness not only diminishes economic growth but also tears at the fabric of our society. America cannot succeed if the basic bargain at the heart of our economy remains broken. The most fortunate among us who have reached the pinnacles of power and success depend on a stable economic and political system. That stability rests on the public's trust that the system operates in the interest of us all. Any loss of such trust threatens the well-being of everyone. We will choose reform, I believe, because we are a sensible nation, and reform is the only sensible option we have.

AFTERWORD

A few years ago Jake Kornbluth, a young filmmaker, came to visit me in my office at Berkeley. He had read *Aftershock* and wanted to base a documentary on it.

I was skeptical. Although the issue of widening inequality had preoccupied me for years, I didn't see how it could be translated onto a movie screen. The topic does not exactly lend itself to action adventure or romantic comedy.

Jake wasn't sure, either. So I suggested he sit in on my large undergraduate class, "Wealth and Poverty," which covers much of the same ground in greater detail. The course gave him some ideas.

Jake worked on the film for the next year and a half. He asked me to do several "shootings" where I spoke directly to the camera, answering questions he came up with. I brought Jake and his crew to labor-union meetings I had been invited to attend, political rallies, speeches, and to meetings with various groups I'd been working with. We traveled together to Washington to interview politicians and others who had some official responsibility for the economy. He and his crew also filmed my Berkeley class in its entirety.

I still had no idea what the film would look like. When anyone inquired, Jake would say it was "'An Inconvenient Truth' on the economy" (referring to Al Gore's movie on climate change), and that I'd be playing Al Gore's role. That worried me. I have nothing but admiration for the former vice president and presidential candidate and for the film he hosted—but I'm no Al Gore. And in comparing our effort to *An Inconvenient Truth*, I thought Jake was setting the bar way too high.

Jake also needed money to make the film. Even the cheapest movie requires people to get the picture and sound right and to edit the film; he also needed archival footage, graphics, and music. Luckily, he found two young producers, Jen Chaiken and Sebastian Dungan, who were eager to help.

Jake and I also went to Kickstarter.com—an online means of presenting new projects and eliciting contributions from people who might want to support them. We set a target of $75,000 and a deadline of just four weeks. It was a tough call because if the target wasn't met, pledged contributions up to that point wouldn't count. We wrote up a short summary of the film project and made a short video describing it. And we included a list of rewards based on the amount pledged. (People who contributed $10 or more would get a thank-you video; $100 or more and their name would be listed on the film credits at the end of the movie; $500 or more would earn them an exclusive screening with the filmmakers; $1000 or more would summon a signed hand-drawn cartoon portrait of the donor, drawn by me!). We put it all up on the Kickstarter webpage, and waited.

I was frankly surprised at the result: over $83,000 in pledges from 1,015 backers. It wasn't everything Jake needed—Jen and Sebastian still had lots of work to do—but it was a great help.

The film debuted at the Sundance Film Festival in January 2013. It had five screenings and got five standing ovations. It also won an award. Harvey Weinstein, the Hollywood impresario, loved the film and wanted to distribute it. Jake, Jen, Sebastian, and I were thrilled.

It seemed possible that the challenge of widening inequality would get the public hearing it needed. That could be a start. The only hope we have for reversing it is an informed public that demands genuine reform.

Robert B. Reich
June 2013

APPENDIX: WHAT'S HAPPENED

Through recoveries and recessions, inequality continues to widen in America. Some inequality is inevitable and desirable. It gives people an incentive to work and invest, from which everyone benefits.

But at some point inequality of income and wealth becomes so wide as to harm society. When almost all the economic gains go to the top, the middle class and everyone aspiring to join it no longer have the purchasing power to keep the economy going. Moreover, with a relatively small number of people owning most of the wealth and accounting for most of investment decisions, the economy is more vulnerable to booms and busts.

As income concentrates at the top, the wealthy also gain disproportionate political power to entrench their wealth through public policies that favor them—policies that reduce their taxes, cut regulations that impose on their profits, enhance government subsidies to them and their enterprises, and reward them with monopolies. Under these circumstances, many people of low or average means cannot get advance, no matter how hard they try.

This degree of inequality harms even the wealthy over the long term. They would do better with a smaller share of a rapidly growing economy than with a large share of an economy that's barely growing and subject to periodic crashes and prolonged downturns. Yet buoyant economic growth isn't possible without a large and growing middle class able to buy what the economy is capable of producing.

The wealthy would also do better in a society whose members readily joined together to solve problems than one rife with dissention and conflict. Yet collaboration is difficult when people feel the game is rigged against them, and that no matter how hard they work they still can't get ahead.

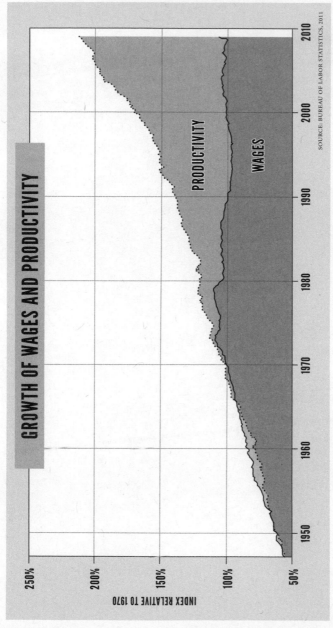

GROWTH OF WAGES AND PRODUCTIVITY

INDEX RELATIVE TO 1970

250%

200%

150%

100%

50%

PRODUCTIVITY

WAGES

1950   1960   1970   1980   1990   2000   2010

SOURCE: BUREAU OF LABOR STATISTICS, 2011

For the first three decades after World War II, the typical worker's earnings (here, average hourly compensation) grew in tandem with gains in productivity. But starting in the late 1970s, the earnings of the typical worker began to flatten, and most of the gain from productivity started going to the top.

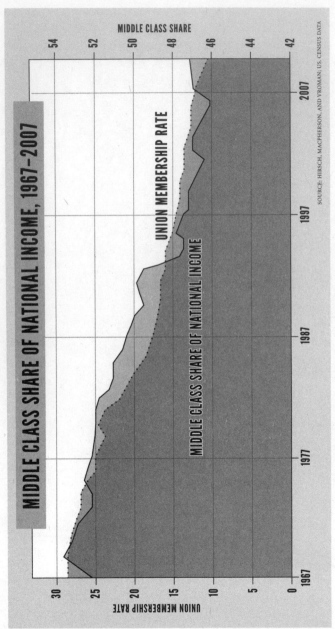

MIDDLE CLASS SHARE OF NATIONAL INCOME, 1967–2007

MIDDLE CLASS SHARE

UNION MEMBERSHIP RATE

MIDDLE CLASS SHARE OF NATIONAL INCOME

UNION MEMBERSHIP RATE

SOURCE: HIRSCH, MACPHERSON, AND VROMAN; US. CENSUS DATA

In the decades after World War II, labor unions had given workers the bargaining power they needed to get a share of national income proportional to their output—and thereby build the middle class. But as union membership declined, the share of national income going to the middle class declined as well.

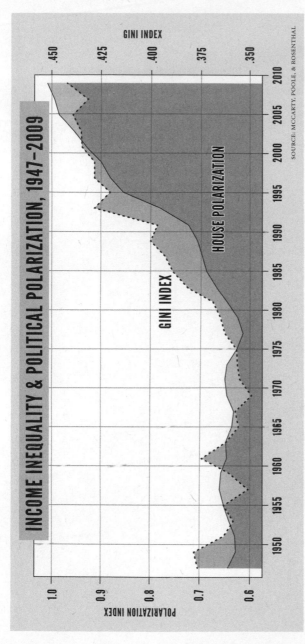

Increasing political polarization—measured as the average distance between Democratic and Republican members of the House of Representatives on a scale of liberal to conservative—directly correlates with widening income inequality. That may be because a majority of Americans, increasingly frustrated and economically insecure, want to blame someone or some group—big government or big business, the poor or the rich, new immigrants or global trade—and political parties facilitate such a blame game.

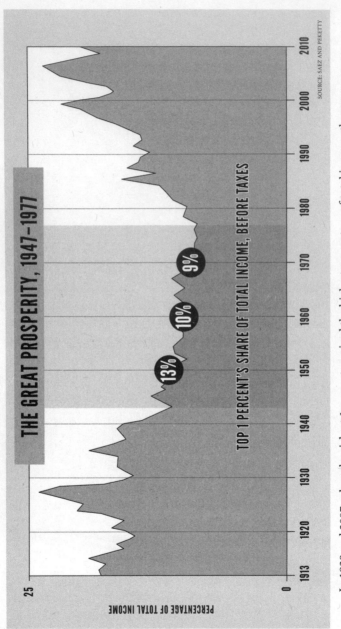

THE GREAT PROSPERITY, 1947–1977

TOP 1 PERCENT'S SHARE OF TOTAL INCOME, BEFORE TAXES

13%   10%   9%

PERCENTAGE OF TOTAL INCOME

25

0

1913 1920 1930 1940 1950 1960 1970 1980 1990 2000 2010

SOURCE: SAEZ AND PEKETTY

In 1928 and 2007, when the richest 1 percent received the highest percentage of total income, the economy was particularly fragile. In each of the following years it collapsed. In the intervening years, when the top 1 percent received a far smaller percentage of total income, everyone's income grew and the economy thrived.

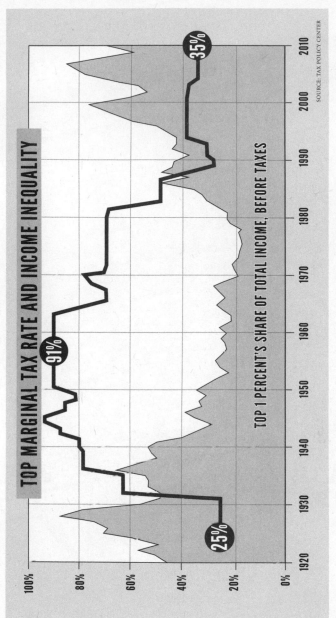

TOP MARGINAL TAX RATE AND INCOME INEQUALITY

91%

35%

25%

TOP 1 PERCENT'S SHARE OF TOTAL INCOME, BEFORE TAXES

100%   80%   60%   40%   20%   0%

1920   1930   1940   1950   1960   1970   1980   1990   2000   2010

SOURCE: TAX POLICY CENTER

When income concentrates at the top—as it did in the late 1920s and again in recent years—the wealthy have enough political clout to reduce their taxes. When income is more equally spread, as it was in the intervening decades, the wealthy pay a higher tax rate, presumably because they have less clout.

Economies are never stagnant. Economic upturns are characterized by a virtuous cycle. Larger-scale virtuous cycles extend over several ups and downs when the dominant trend of an era is rapid growth, rising wages, and low unemployment—as it was during the Great Prosperity of the 1950s, 1960s, and early 1970s.

THE VIRTUOUS CYCLE

COMPANIES HIRE MORE
WORKERS BUY MORE
WAGES INCREASE
PRODUCTIVITY GROWS
ECONOMY EXPANDS
WORKERS ARE BETTER EDUCATED
GOVERNMENT INVESTS MORE
TAX REVENUES INCREASE

Economic downturns are characterized by a vicious cycle. Larger-scale vicious cycles extend over several ups and downs when the dominant trend of an era is slow growth, stagnant wages, and high unemployment—as it is today.

THE VICIOUS CYCLE

UNEMPLOYMENT RISES

DEFICITS GROW

WAGES STAGNATE

WORKERS BUY LESS

COMPANIES DOWNSIZE

TAX REVENUES DECREASE

GOVERNMENT CUTS PROGRAMS

WORKERS ARE LESS EDUCATED

ACKNOWLEDGMENTS

This book is the result of discussions with people too numerous to name, although some will no doubt recognize their arguments and counterarguments in these pages. Special mention should go to my former colleagues Jack Donahue and Richard Parker and current colleagues George Akerlof, Brad DeLong, Jack Glaser, David Kirp, Jane Mauldon, Harley Shaiken, Eugene Smolensky, and Laura Tyson, all of whom helped me sharpen my arguments but none of whom should bear responsibility for them. Several friends subjected earlier drafts to the sort of criticism only friends can be trusted to provide. Here, Doug Dworkin, John Isaacson, and Erik Tarloff played their customary roles. I am also grateful to diligent students here at the Goldman School of Public Policy, especially to Mia Bird, Teal Brown, Jason Burwen, Jonathan Stein, and Renee Willette, who helped me trace down facts and focus the argument. The Blum Center and the Goldman School, both at the University of California at Berkeley, provided financial support. As usual, my assistant, Rebecca Boles, was extraordinarily helpful, and Manuel Castrillo was responsive to all calls for technical assistance. I want to give special thanks to my partner, Perian Flaherty, for her remarkable insight, editorial flair, patience, and ever wise judgment. My agent, Rafe Sagalyn, provided much needed advice, and my long-standing editor and friend, Jonathan Segal, offered abiding encouragement, wisdom, and thoughtfulness.

NOTES

INTRODUCTION. THE PENDULUM

2   Our history swings much like a pendulum: On this point, see Arthur M. Schlesinger, Jr., *The Cycles of American History* (New York: Houghton Mifflin, 1986). Schlesinger defined a political-economic cycle as "a continuing shift in national involvement between public purpose and private interest" (p. 27). See also Albert O. Hirschman, *Shifting Involvements: Private Interest and Public Action* (Princeton, N.J.: Princeton University Press, 1982).

5   the last time income was this concentrated: See Thomas Piketty and Emmanuel Saez, "The Evolution of Top Incomes: A Historical and International Perspective," *AEA Papers and Proceedings* 96, no. 2 (May 2006): 200–205.

PART I. The Broken Bargain
1. ECCLES'S INSIGHT

12   "Men I respected assured me": All quotes in this chapter are from Marriner Eccles's memoir, *Beckoning Frontiers* (New York: Alfred A. Knopf, 1951), pp. 54, 71–81.

2. PARALLELS

19   The wages of the typical American: See Bureau of Economic Analysis, National Compensation Survey, "Current-Dollar Historical Listings: Employee Cost Listings Historical Index," Tables 4–10, January 2010.

19   a male worker earning the median male wage: See U.S. Census Bureau press release, "Household Income Rises, Poverty Rate Unchanged, Number of Uninsured Down," U.S. Census Bureau, Current Population Survey data, August 26, 2008.

19   Economists Emmanuel Saez and Thomas Piketty: See Thomas Picketty and Emmanuel Saez, "The Evolution of Top Incomes: A Historical and International Perspective," *AEA Papers and Proceedings* 96, no. 2 (May

2006): 200–205. The most recent update of their data can be found in Emmanuel Saez, "Striking It Richer: The Evolution of Top Incomes in the United States," University of California, Department of Economics, August 5, 2009. Their calculation is before paying taxes, and it includes income from capital gains.

20 Sociologists Robert S. Lynd and his wife: See Robert S. Lynd and Helen Merrell Lynd, *Middletown* (New York: Harcourt Brace, 1929), pp. 21–24.

23 Savings had averaged 9–10 percent of after-tax income: See Bureau of Economic Analysis, National Income and Product Accounts Table, "Personal Income and Its Distribution," last updated January 29, 2010 (http://www.bea.gov/national/nipaweb/TableView.asp?SelectedTable =58&ViewSeries=NO&Java=no&Request3Place=N&3Place=N&From View=YES&Freq=Year&FirstYear=1943&LastYear=2009&3Place=N& Update=Update&JavaBox=no#Mid).

23 Total mortgage debt was almost three times higher: See ibid.

23 The Dow Jones Industrial Average: See Dow Jones Industrial Average Historical Charts, daily, Thomson Reuters and IDC/ComStock (http://stockcharts.com/charts/historical/djia19201940.html).

24 Four years later: See *Stock Exchange Practices*, Hearings, April–June 1932, Part 2, pp. 566–67.

25 Meanwhile, National City Bank: See Federal Deposit Insurance Corporation, "Learning Bank" http://www.fdic.gov/about/learn/learning/when/1930s.html.

3. THE BASIC BARGAIN

28 On January 5, 1914, Henry Ford: See A. Rees, National Bureau of Economic Research, *Real Wages in Manufacturing 1890 to 1914*, Chapter 5, "Real Wages," 1961 (http://www.nber.org/books/rees61-1).

28 Ford was . . . a smart capitalist: See A. Nevins and F. Ernest Hill, *Ford: The Times, the Man, the Company* (New York: Scribners, 1954).

29 By the first decades of the twentieth century: See Damon Silvers, "How a Low Wage Economy with Weak Labor Laws Brought Us the Mortgage Credit Crisis," lecture presented by *The Berkeley Journal of Employment and Labor Law*, Institute of Research on Labor and Employment, University of California, Berkeley, April 2, 2008 (http://www.irle.berkeley.edu/events/spring08/feller/).

29 British economist John Maynard Keynes: These and subsequent quotes from John Maynard Keynes, *The General Theory of Employment, Interest and Money* (New York: Harcourt Brace, 1936), pp. 373–74.

30 "Liquidate labor, liquidate stocks": See Herbert Hoover, *The Memoirs of*

Herbert Hoover, vol. 3: *The Great Depression 1929–1941* (New York: Macmillan, 1952).

4. HOW CONCENTRATED INCOME AT THE TOP HURTS THE ECONOMY

32 The richest man in the world: See "Richest in the World, 2008," *Forbes* magazine (http://www.forbes.com/lists/2008/10/billionaires08_Warren -Buffett_CoR3.html).

32 in the same gray stucco house: See Roger Lowenstein, *Buffett: The Making of an American Capitalist* (New York: Broadway Books, 1995), pp. 8–10.

33 "If I wanted to," Buffet once said: See Janet Lowe, *Warren Buffett Speaks: Wit and Wisdom from the World's Greatest Investor* (New York: John Wiley & Sons, 1997), pp. 165–66.

33 the nearly $100 million Kenneth Lewis earned: See Securities and Exchange Commission Filings compiled by *Forbes* magazine, *CEO Compensation Reports* (sources: Bank of America SEC Filings; FT Interactive Data; and LionShares via FactSet Research Systems).

33 In the year prior to Lehman Brothers': See ibid.

35 Taxing the wealthy to help the poor: See Jeremy Bentham, "Critique of the Doctrine of Inalienable, Natural Rights," in *Anarchical Fallacies,* vol. 2 of *The Works of Jeremy Bentham,* ed. John Bowring (Edinburgh: William Tait, 1843).

36 the top 10 percent took home: See analysis by Lawrence Mishel, Jared Bernstein, and Heidi Shierholz, *The State of Working America, 2008/ 2009,* Chapter 5, Table 2.4, "Shares of Total Income (Before and After Tax) and Income Tax for Percentile Groups" (Washington, D.C.: Economic Policy Institute, 2010).

37 "much lower stakes will serve": John Maynard Keynes, *The General Theory of Employment, Interest and Money* (London: Macmillan, 1961), p. 374.

5. WHY POLICYMAKERS OBSESS ABOUT THE FINANCIAL ECONOMY INSTEAD OF ABOUT THE REAL ONE

38 "Without this rescue plan": See "White House Written Statement of President George W. Bush," September 28, 2009 (http://thepage.time .com/statement-by-president-bush/).

38 "If we do not do this": Senator Judd Gregg to the Associated Press, September 28, 2008.

41 The relative calm of preceding decades: The theoretical underpinnings

of this occurrence had been developed by economist Hyman Minsky. See Hyman Minsky, *Stabilizing an Unstable Economy* (New York: McGraw-Hill, 2008).

6. THE GREAT PROSPERITY: 1947–1975

43 During this quarter century: See U.S. Census Bureau, Current Population Reports, *Measuring 50 Years of Economic Change Using the March Current Population Survey* (U.S. Government Printing Office, Washington, D.C., 1998), pp. 7–8.

43 Labor productivity: U.S. Bureau of Labor Statistics, Historical SIC Industry Labor and Cost Indexes, 1947–1977.

43 Expressed in 2007 dollars: See U.S. Bureau of Labor Statistics Series Reports, "Family, All Races by Median and Mean Income: 1947 to 2006," Table F-7 (http://www.census.gov/hhes/www/income/histinc/f07ar .html).

44 By the end of the war: See Budget of the United States Government, Historical Tables, Federal Debt, Table 7.1—Federal Debt at the End of Year: 1940–2013, Executive Office of the President, December 2008.

44 "All alike expect and fear": Alvin Hansen, *Economic Problems of the Post War World: Democratic Planning for Full Employment,* National Council for the Social Studies, 1942.

45 By the mid-1950s: See "Union Members Summary," U.S. Bureau of Labor Statistics economic news release, January 2010 (http://www.bls .gov/news.release/union2.nr0.htm).

45 "Unless we get a more realistic distribution": See Nelson Lichtenstein, *Walter Reuther: The Most Dangerous Man in Detroit* (New York: Basic Books, 1995), p. 231.

46 A college sociology textbook of 1956: See Joseph Kahl, *The American Class Structure* (New York: Holt, Rinehart, 1956), pp. 109–10.

47 The interstate highway system: See Richard Weingroff, *The Greatest Decade: 1956 to 1966,* Federal Highway Commission Report, December 22, 2008.

47 The expansion of public universities: See U.S. Census Bureau, Current Population Survey, Annual Social and Economic Supplements, "Type of Family, All Races by Median and Mean Income: 1947 to 2006" (http://www.census.gov/hhes/www/income/histinc/f07ar.html).

47 The federal government, especially the Defense Department: See U.S. Department of Education, National Center for Education Statistics, *Digest of Education Statistics, 2008* (NCES 2009–020), Chapter 3, 2009.

48 The Pentagon also gave birth: See M. H. Weik, "The ENIAC Story," Ordinance Ballistic Research Laboratories, 1961.

48 New fighter jets and engines morphed: See Boeing Airlines, "Commercial Airplanes: Military Derivatives," Boeing Airlines External Communications Commercial Airline Division (http://www.boeing.com/ commercial/707family/deriv.html).

48 "The old imperialism": Inaugural address of President Harry S. Truman, January 20, 1949.

49 In the 1950s, under President Dwight Eisenhower: See Internal Revenue Service, Statistics of Income, Individual Statistical Tables by Tax Rate and Income Percentile.

50 "a better, richer, and happier life": James Truslow Adams, *The Epic of America* (Boston: Little, Brown, 1931), p. 73.

7. HOW WE GOT OURSELVES INTO THE SAME MESS AGAIN

51 By the late 1990s: See U.S. Census Bureau, "Historical Trends in Income Inequality—Middle Class," Table H-3, "Historical Income Tables by Quintile."

53 the median wage flattened: See U.S. Census Bureau, "Historical Trends in Income Inequality—Middle Class," Table H-3.

55 It shredded safety nets: See U.S. Department of Labor, Workforce Security Data Tables, "Unemployment Insurance Data Tables: 1st Quarter–4th Quarter, 2007," Division of Actuarial Resources, Office of Income Support, January 7, 2010.

56 by 2010, fewer than 8 percent: See U.S. Bureau of Labor Statistics economic news release, "Union Members Summary—2009," January 22, 2010.

56 And nothing impeded CEO salaries: See Lawrence Mishel, "Executive Pay," in *The State of Working America* (Washington, D.C.: Economic Policy Institute, 2008), pp. 220–24.

56 More than half of all the money: See Lawrence Bebchuk, "The Growth of Executive Pay," *Oxford Review of Economic Policy* 21, no. 2 (2005): 283–303.

56 By 2007, financial and insurance companies: See Bureau of Economic Analysis, National Income and Product Accounts (NIPA) Tables, Section I: Domestic Product and Incomes, "Real Gross Value Added by Industry," 2009.

57 In 2009, the twenty-five best-paid hedge-fund managers: See *AR: Absolute Return + Alpha*, annual survey, 2009.

57 in 2007, Ford's financial division: Securities and Exchange Commission Filings.

58 according to presidential candidate Ronald Reagan: Ronald Reagan campaign address, "A Vital Economy: Jobs, Growth, and Progress for Americans," October 24, 1980.

60 Moreover, they had no clear memory: See *Technology Triumphs, Morality Falters,* Section 5: "America's Collective Memory," the Pew Research Center for the People and the Press, January 3, 1999.

8. HOW AMERICANS KEPT BUYING ANYWAY: THE THREE COPING MECHANISMS

61 Coping mechanism #1: See U.S. Department of Labor Women's Bureau, "Labor Force Participation of Women and Mothers," Historical Data Tables, October 9, 2009 (http://www.bls.gov/opub/ted/2009/ted_2009 1009.htm).

62 Coping mechanism #2: See U.S. Bureau of Labor Statistics, 2008 American Time Use Survey, "Working and Work Related Activities Tables," 2008 (http://www.bls.gov/tus/current/work.htm).

62 Coping mechanism #3: See Bureau of Economic Analysis, National Income and Product Accounts Table 2.1, "Personal Income and Its Distribution," January 29, 2010 (http://www.bea.gov/national/nipaweb/ TableView.asp?SelectedTable=58&Freq=Qtr&FirstYear=2007&LastYear =2009).

63 in 1980 the average home: See U.S. Census Bureau, "Median and Average Home Sales Prices, Annual Historical Data," December 2, 2004.

9. THE FUTURE WITHOUT COPING MECHANISMS

67 In 2009, some 50 million workers: See A. Munnell, J. P. Aubrey, and D. Muldoon, *The Financial Crisis and Private Defined Benefit Plans,* Center for Retirement Research at Boston College, November 8, 2008.

68 "should have enough spending power": See Bank of America Merrill Lynch, *The Myth of the Overleveraged Consumer,* August 14, 2009.

10. WHY CHINA WON'T SAVE US

69 "We cannot go back": Barack Obama, "G-20 Summit in Pittsburgh: Obama's First UN Address, HIV Vaccine in the Works," transcript provided by CNN, September 24, 2009.

70 By 2009, China was second only to the United States: See Bank of America Merrill Lynch, *US Economics Weekly,* Merrill Lynch Global Research, Products and Reports, October 2009.

70 But the benefits of China's growth: See Barry Ritholtz, "China Con-

sumer Spending vs. Saving," May 8, 2009 (http://www.ritholtz.com/blog/2009/05/china-consumer-spending-vs-savings/). Data sources: Bank of America Merrill Lynch, "United States Economics, 2009."

72 In 2009, other American firms: See General Motors, Evergreen Solar, and General Electric press releases, 2008 to 2010.

PART II. Backlash

2. THE POLITICS OF ECONOMICS, 2010–2020

84 Just before the Great Recession: See Bureau of Economic Analysis, National Income and Product Accounts Tables, Table 1.5.5: Gross Domestic Product, Expanded Detail. Last revised: January 29, 2010.

84 Personal consumption did not always constitute 70 percent: See Bureau of Economic Analysis, National Income and Product Accounts Tables, Table 1.5.5.

3. WHY CAN'T WE BE CONTENT WITH LESS?

85 "Many of the so-called comforts of life": Henry David Thoreau, *Walden; or, Life in the Woods* (Boston: Ticknor and Fields, 1854), p. 15.

85 "The people of this country need": John S. Ellsworth, Jr., "The Depression Generation," *The North American Review* 234 (October 1932).

85 University of Michigan researcher Ronald Inglehart: See Ronald Inglehart, Christian Welzel, and Roberto Foa, *World Values Survey: Happiness Trends in 24 Countries, 1946–2006*, January 2008.

86 In 1943, behavioral scientist Abraham Maslow: The original article appeared in *Psychological Review* 50, no. 4 (1943): 370–96. See also Janet Simons, Donald Irwin, and Beverly Drinnien, *Psychology: The Search for Understanding* (New York: West Publishing Company, 1987).

86 Before the Great Recession: See press release: *Annals of Internal Medicine,* University of Chicago Medical School Press, December 6, 2004.

86 In 2007, Americans spent a whopping $23.9 billion: J. LaRosa, "U.S. Sleep Aids Market Now Worth $23 Billion as Americans Battle Insomnia, Sleep Disorders," Marketdata Enterprises press release, June 2008.

87 In mid-2009, the *Archives of General Psychiatry:* See Mark Olfson and Steven C. Marcus, "National Patterns in Antidepressant Medication Treatment," *Archives of General Psychiatry,* 66, no. 8 (August 2009): 848–56.

87 "through the whole of his life": Adam Smith, *Theory of Moral Sentiments* (London: A. Millar Publishing, 1790), pp. 261–63.

88 Almost 10 percent fewer people were killed: See National Highway Traffic Safety Administration Fatality Analysis Reporting System Encyclopedia (http://www-fars.nhtsa.dot.gov/Main/index.aspx).

88 deaths and serious injuries dropped: See U.S. Bureau of Labor Statistics, economic news release: "Workplace Injury and Illness Summary," October 29, 2009.

4. THE PAIN OF ECONOMIC LOSS

90 Princeton psychologist Daniel Kahneman: See D. Kahneman, J. L. Knetch, and R. H. Thaler, "Anomalies: The Endowment Effect, Loss Aversion, and Status Quo Bias," *Journal of Economic Perspectives*, 5, no. 1 (Winter 1991): 193–206.

90 Societies whose living standards drop: Ibid.

90 Behavioral economist Christopher Ruhm: See C. J. Ruhm, *Are Recessions Good for Your Health?*, National Bureau of Economic Research, March 2006.

90 The stock market crash of 1929: See Leonardo Tondo and Ross J. Baldessarini, *Suicides: Causes and Clinical Management*, Medscape Medical News (http://cme.medscape.com/viewarticle/413195_2).

91 "the crisis quality of a serious illness": Robert S. Lynd and Helen Merrell Lynd, *Middletown in Transition: A Study in Cultural Conflicts* (New York: Harcourt Brace, 1937), p. 489.

5. ADDING INSULT TO INJURY

93 The median pay of CEOs: See American Federation of Labor and Congress of Industrial Organizations, Executive Paywatch Database, "CEO Pay Rates," 2008.

94 According to *The New York Times:* See Graham Bowley, "Strong Year for Goldman as It Trims Bonus Pool," *New York Times,* January 21, 2010.

95 "In a poor society a man proves": See R. Layard, "Human Satisfactions and Public Policy," *Economic Journal* 90, no. 360 (December 1980): 737–50.

95 Adam Smith defined necessities: See Adam Smith, *An Enquiry into the Nature and Causes of Wealth and Nations* (London: Methuen, 1776), Book 5, Chapter 2.

96 In 1899, the economist-sociologist Thorstein Veblen: Thorstein Veblen, *The Theory of the Leisure Class* (New York: Macmillan, 1899). See Ken McCormick, "Veblen and Duesenberry: The Demonstration Effect Revisited," *Journal of Economic Issues* 17, no. 4 (December 1983): 1125–29.

96 More than a half century later: James Duesenberry, *Income, Saving and*

the Theory of Consumer Behavior, Harvard Economic Studies, 1967. For a highly pertinent and thoughtful treatment of this subject, see Robert H. Frank, *Falling Behind: How Rising Inequality Harms the Middle Class* (Berkeley: University of California Press, 2007).

96 "Wealth . . . is any income at least $100 more a year": H. L. Mencken, *A Book of Burlesques,* (New York: Alfred A. Knopf, 1916), p. 310.

97 the typical new home built in the United States in 2007: See Gopal Ahluwahlia, *National Association of Home Builders: Consumer Preferences,* February 14, 2008.

98 *The Daily Beast* reported that Kathleen Fuld: See "What the Rich Don't Want You to Know About the Way They Spend Their Money," *Daily Beast,* December 5, 2008.

98 Prestigious universities have only a limited number: Pell Grants, available only to students whose families are relatively poor, offer one measure. In 2006 (the most recent year for which data is available), just one in ten Harvard students received a Pell Grant. Other of America's elite universities have similar percentages. See http://www.jbhe.com/features/57_pellgrants.html. By way of comparison, at most campuses of the University of California, a public institution, approximately 30 percent of students are eligible for Pell Grants.

100 economists Roberto Perotti and Alberto Alesina have found: A. Alesina and R. Perotti, "Income Distribution, Political Instability, and Investment," *European Economic Review* 40 (June, 1996): 1202–29.

6. OUTRAGE AT A RIGGED GAME

101 But when the *San Francisco Chronicle* reported: Nanette Asimov, "Execs Still Get Raises as UC Cuts Staffing Pay," *San Francisco Chronicle,* August 7, 2009.

104 in a poll taken by Hart Associates: Hart Associates poll of 802 voters taken September 21–23, 2009, http://epi.3cdn.net/e5566d3b8ac34f6079_yym6bxts7.pdf).

105 The inspector general concluded: "Factors Affecting Efforts to Limit Payments to AIG Counterparties," Office of the Special Inspector General for the Troubled Asset Relief Program, November 17, 2009 (http://www.sigtarp.gov/reports/audit/2009/Factors_Affecting_Efforts_to_Limit_Payments_to_AIG_Counterparties.pdf).

105 "If banks had cut mortgage rates": Peter Eavis, "U.S. Aids Benefits Banks, Not Homeowners," *Wall Street Journal,* January 19, 2010.

107 During the 2008 elections: Data on lobbying expenditures and campaign contributions are available at the industry-specific level from OpenSecrets.org. The data for "Finance/Insurance/Real Estate," for

example, is available at http://www.opensecrets.org/industries/indus.php?ind=F.

110 According to the Center for Public Integrity: "More Than 2,000 Spin Through Revolving Door," LobbyWatch, Center for Public Integrity, May 2, 2006 (http://projects.publicintegrity.org/lobby/report.aspx?aid=678).

110 When Dick Gephardt ran for president in 1988: Sebastian Jones, "Dick Gephardt's Spectacular Sellout," *The Nation*, September 30, 2009 (http://www.thenation.com/doc/20091019/jones).

112 Between 2012 and 2021: "The Estate Tax: Myths and Realities," Center on Budget and Policy Priorities, February 23, 2009 (http://www.cbpp.org/files/estatetaxmyths.pdf).

7. THE POLITICS OF ANGER

116 One, nicknamed "Jackpot Jimmy": James Barron and Russ Buettner, "Scorn Trails A.I.G. Executives, Even in Their Driveways," *New York Times*, March 19, 2009.

117 In a poll taken in December 2009: "U.S. Seen as Less Important, China as More Powerful," Survey Reports, Pew Research Center for the People and the Press, December 3, 2009.

118 Tom Tancredo, a former congressman: Adam Nagourney, "Conservatives Get a Look at Possible Candidates, *New York Times*, February 20, 2010.

118 Governor Tim Pawlenty: Quoted in "Scenes from a Counter-Revolution," *The Economist*, February 13, 2010, p. 31.

118 "get rid of the power people": Kate Zernike, "Paul Vows to Remain True to the Tea Party," *New York Times*, May 18, 2010.

119 "heading in the wrong direction": Wall Street Journal/NBC News poll taken December 9–13, 2010.

119 "The wizards in Washington": Chuck Baldwin, "Anger with Government Not Enough," Independent Political Report, December 18, 2009 (http://www.independentpoliticalreport.com/2009/12/chuck-baldwin-anger-with-federal-government-not-enough/).

119 It was the bailout of Wall Street: Quoted in Gerald Seib, "No Seat for Wall Street at Tea Party, *Wall Street Journal*, January 12, 2010.

119 Historian Richard Hofstadter: Richard Hofstadter, "The Paranoid Style in American Politics," *Harper's Magazine*, November 1964, pp. 77–86.

121 Father Charles Coughlin of Detroit: A collection of Father Coughlin's speeches, including the one quoted here, can be found on the Social Security Administration's Web site: http://www.ssa.gov/history/fcspeech.html.

121 Senator Huey "the Kingfish" Long of Louisiana: Information about Huey Long and his populist politics is also available on the Social Security Administration's Web site: http://www.ssa.gov/history/hlong1 .html.

122 A classic sociological study of thirty-five dictatorships: J. O. Hertzler, "Crises and Dictatorships," *American Sociological Review* 5 (1940): 157–69.

PART III. The Bargain Restored

1. WHAT SHOULD BE DONE: A NEW DEAL FOR THE MIDDLE CLASS

130 The yearly cost to the federal government: This sum is calculated by multiplying Census data on the number of people in each income category (<$20K, $20K–$30K, etc.) by the average income supplement awarded in that category. We assume an even distribution of incomes in each bracket.

130 If initially set at $35 per metric ton: See Ian W. H. Parry, "Should the Obama Administration Implement a CO2 Tax?," Resources for the Future, Issue Brief #09-05, April 2009. Also, "Energy Market Impacts of Alternative Greenhouse Gas Intensity Reduction Goals," Energy Information Administration, SR/OIAF/2006-01, 2006. Numbers have been adjusted to 2008 dollars and emissions. Note that these estimates are based on an analysis of pricing of safety-valve permits under a cap-and-trade system—which is, in effect, setting a carbon tax at the margin and effectively produces a ceiling on tradable permit prices. Safety-valve prices would also increase 5 percent in nominal terms annually. Also note that this is a comparison to a reference "business-as-usual" case—the analyzed values do not actually reduce emissions below current levels; only the highest-price scenario keeps emissions stable. Thus, an alternate wording for the above scenario would be: "If set initially at $35 per ton of carbon dioxide equivalent, a carbon tax would raise $210 billion in annual revenue at the outset and would put the United States on a path to reduce emissions by 14 percent by 2020 (28 percent in 2030) compared to a business-as-usual scenario."

130 By the time it reached $115 per ton: James Hansen, "Cap and Fade," *New York Times,* December 6, 2009.

131 people in the top 1 percent: "Summary of Latest Federal Individual Income Tax Data, 1980–2007," Tax Data, Tax Foundation, July 30, 2009. Also, "SOI Tax Stats—Individual Statistical Tables by Tax Rate and Income Percentile," Internal Revenue Service, IRS.gov.

131 would raise $600 billion more: The total revenue generated by this for-
mulation of the tax code was calculated using IRS data on the number
of taxpayers in each income bracket and the total value of federal
income taxes paid by all members of that bracket. Those figures were
combined to determine the average salary of each bracket, which was
then assessed in a marginal fashion at the rates included herein. The
total taxes paid by the average earner in each income bracket was then
multiplied by the number of earners in that earner's respective bracket.
Federal income tax revenue generated the following amounts. Among
$50–$160K: $199 billion. Among $160–$260K: $254.9 billion. Among
$260–$410K: $123.8 billion. Among $410K+: $974.1 billion. (All revenue
generated by Americans earning less than $50,00 was removed.) Total
generated in federal income taxes: $1,551.8 billion. Total generated
under current federal income tax system: $1,115.5 billion. Net: $436.3 billion. A similar analysis was done for capital gains taxes, yielding a net of
some $170 billion.

131 The four hundred highest-income taxpayers in 2007: See David Cay
Johnston, *Tax Analysts*, http://www.tax.com/taxcom/.../0DEC0EAA7E
4D7A2B852576CD00714692.

132 from 1936 to 1980, the top marginal tax rate: "U.S. Individual Income
Tax: Personal Exemptions and Lowest and Highest Bracket Tax Rates
and Tax Base for Regular Tax," SOI Bulletin Historical Table 23, Internal
Revenue Service.

132 the effective rate, after all deductions and credits: Roberton Williams,
"Who Pays Federal Taxes?," Tax Policy Center, April 2009.

136 Children in these programs are more likely to graduate: James J. Heck-
man and Dimitriy V. Masterov, "The Productivity Argument for Investing in Young Children," T. W. Schultz Award Lecture at the Allied Social
Sciences Association annual meeting, Chicago, January 5–7, 2007. See
also Janet Currie, "Early Childhood Education Programs," *Journal of
Economic Perspectives* 15, no. 2 (Spring 2001): 213–38; Ron Haskins and
Cecilia Rouse, "Closing Achievement Gaps," The Future of Children,
policy brief, Spring 2005.

136 A total of $20 billion per year: A recent Brookings Institution study by
Julia B. Isaacs ("Supporting Young Children and Families: An Investment Strategy That Pays") found that full-spectrum early childhood
care and education would cost $18 billion per year.

136 In 2009, about two-thirds of incoming college students: Survey of
220,00 incoming students at 297 campuses, weighed to represent the
1.4 million full-time first-year students who entered colleges and universities in the fall of 2009. The survey was done by the Cooperative
Institutional Research Program, University of California at Los Angeles.

137 The most efficient way: See Sara R. Collins, Jennifer L. Nicholson, and Sheila D. Rustgi, "An Analysis of Leading Congressional Health Care Bills, 2007–2008: Part I, Insurance Coverage," The Commonwealth Fund, January 9, 2009.

138 A study by the Harvard Medical School: Steffie Woolhandler et al., "Costs of Health Administration in the United States and Canada," *New England Journal of Medicine* 349, no. 8 (August 21, 2003): 768–75.

138 Medicare's administrative costs: Cathy Schoen et al., "Building Blocks for Reform: Achieving Universal Coverage with Private and Public Group Health Insurance," *Health Affairs* 27, no. 3 (May/June 2008): 647.

138 the Congressional Budget Office has found: Congressional Budget Office, "Designing a Premium Support System for Medicare," November 2006, p. 12.

138 In a poll conducted for NBC News: The poll can be found at http://msnbcmedia.msn./i/msnbc/sections/news/090617_NBC-WSJ_poll_Full.pdf.

139 dramatically reduce traffic congestion: "Assessing the Full Costs of Congestion on Surface Transportation Systems and Reducing Them Through Pricing," U.S. Department of Transportation, 2009.

INDEX

Page numbers in *italic* refer to figures.

BEYOND OUTRAGE

*What Has Gone Wrong with Our Economy
and Our Democracy, and How to Fix It*

America's economy and democracy are working for the benefit of an ever-fewer privileged and powerful people. In this timely book, Robert B. Reich argues that nothing good happens in Washington unless citizens are energized and organized to make sure Washington acts in the public good. The first step is to see the big picture. *Beyond Outrage* connects the dots, showing why the increasing share of income and wealth going to the top has hobbled jobs and growth for everyone else, undermining our democracy; caused Americans to become increasingly cynical about public life; and turned many Americans against one another. He also explains why the proposals of the "regressive right" are dead wrong and provides a clear roadmap of what must be done instead. Here's a plan for action for everyone who cares about the future of America.

Politics

THE FUTURE OF SUCCESS

Working and Living in the New Economy

Americans may be earning more than ever before, but they're paying a steep price: they're working longer and seeing their families less, and their communities are fragmenting. With clarity and insight, Robert B. Reich delineates what success has come to mean in modern times. Although people have more choices as consumers and investors, these choices are undermining the rest of their lives. It is getting harder for them to be confident of what they will earn next year, or even next month. These trends are powerful but not irreversible, and Reich makes provocative suggestions for a more balanced society and more satisfying lives.

Business

LOCKED IN THE CABINET

In this compelling memoir, former Secretary of Labor Robert B. Reich debunks and demystifies Washington as never before. He honors the much-maligned civil servants who make government work and skewers the politicians who bring it to a halt. He tells us what he and Bill Clinton dreamed of achieving and why some of those dreams didn't come true. Never has a presidential administration been chronicled with such wit and warmth, or its triumphs and failures assessed with such exuberant candor.

Autobiography

REASON
Why Liberals Will Win the Battle for America

In the pages of *Reason*, Reich mounts a defense of classic liberalism that's also a guide for rolling back twenty years of radical conservative domination of our politics and political culture. Reich shows how liberals can shift the focus of the values debate from behavior in the bedroom to malfeasance in the boardroom, and reclaim patriotism from those who equate it with preemptive war-making and the suppression of dissent.

Politics

SUPERCAPITALISM
The Transformation of Business, Democracy, and Everyday Life

From one of America's foremost economic and political thinkers comes a vital analysis of our new hypercompetitive and turbo-charged global economy and the effect it is having on American democracy. With his customary wit and insight, Reich shows how widening inequality of income and wealth, heightened job insecurity, and corporate corruption are merely the logical results of a system in which politicians are more beholden to the influence of business lobbyists than to the voters who elected them.

Politics

THE RESURGENT LIBERAL
And Other Unfashionable Prophecies

In *The Resurgent Liberal*, one of the most tough-minded bearers of the torch of liberalism not only champions a cause but looks fairly and unblinkingly at the opposition. Robert B. Reich carefully examines the four "parables" conservatives have exploited to monopolize American politics and outlines what liberals must do to take it back.

Political Science

THE WORK OF NATIONS

There is no longer such a thing as an American economy, says Robert B. Reich. What does it mean to be a nation when money, goods, and services know no borders? And how can our country best ensure that *all* citizens have a share in the new global economy? Reich defines the real challenge facing the United States in this trailblazing book. Original, readable, and vastly informed, *The Work of Nations* is certain to set the standard for the next generation of policy-makers.

Economics

VINTAGE BOOKS
Available wherever books are sold.
www.vintagebooks.com